# Working with Involuntary Clients

# Working with Involuntary Clients

## A guide to practice
## 2nd edition

### Chris Trotter

Los Angeles | London | New Delhi
Singapore | Washington DC

© Chris Trotter 2006

First published in 2006 by
Allen & Unwin Pty Ltd.
83 Alexander St
Crows Nest NSW 2065
Australia

Reprinted 2007, 2008, 2009, 2010, 2011, 2012

SAGE Publications Ltd
1 Oliver's Yard
55 City Road
London EC1Y 1SP

SAGE Publications Inc.
2455 Teller Road
Thousand Oaks, California 91320

SAGE Publications India Pvt Ltd
B 1/I 1 Mohan Cooperative Industrial Area
Mathura Road
New Delhi 110 044

SAGE Publications Asia-Pacific Pte Ltd
3 Church Street
#10-04 Samsung Hub
Singapore 049483

British Library Cataloguing in Publication data
A catalogue record for this book is available from the British Library

ISBN: 978-1-4129-1880-0 (hbk)
ISBN: 978-1-4129-1881-7 (pbk)

Library of Congress Control Number 2005931206

Typeset in 10.5/13.5 Caslon 540 Roman by Bookhouse, Sydney
Printed and bound by CPI Group (UK) Ltd, Croydon, CR0 4YY
Printed on paper from sustainable resources

# CONTENTS

Acknowledgments        viii

**1  Introduction**    1
Who are involuntary clients?    2
The dual role of workers with involuntary clients    3
Direct practice    5
Sources of knowledge in work with involuntary clients    6
Evidence-based practice    8
The purpose of this book    15
The structure of the book    16

**2  What works and what doesn't?**    18
Approaches that work    21
Approaches that sometimes work    31
Approaches that don't work    53
An evidence-based practice model    54
Research evidence, theory and other practice models    55
Summary    63

**3  Role clarification**                                              65
Dual role: Social control and helping                      67
What is negotiable and what is not?                     69
Confidentiality                                                         71
Case manager, case planner or problem-solver?   73
The client's expectations                                       74
Helping the client to understand the nature of
    the professional relationship                       76
Organisational expectations                                   78
Theoretical approach to the work                          79
Case examples                                                         79
Summary                                                                 85

**4  Promoting pro-social outcomes**                          87
Identifying pro-social comments and actions        89
Providing rewards                                                    91
Modelling pro-social behaviours                            93
Challenging undesirable behaviours                       95
Advantages of the pro-social approach                  98
Criticisms of the pro-social approach                    98
Summary                                                                108

**5  Problem-solving**                                                109
Steps in the problem-solving process                   110
Problem-solving, risk assessment and case planning   124
Criticisms of a problem-solving approach             130
Summary                                                                140

**6  The relationship**                                               142
Empathy                                                                  143
Optimism                                                                147
Humour                                                                   149
Self-disclosure                                                        152
Client violence                                                        154
Summary                                                                157

**7   Working with families**                                          158
   When is it appropriate to work with family groups?   159
   Collaborative family counselling                     161
   A home-based model                                   162
   The collaborative family counselling process         163
   Pro-social modelling                                 173
   The worker–client relationship                       174
   Summary                                              180

**8   Evaluation**                                                     181
   Single case study evaluation                         183
   Case analysis                                        187
   Conclusion                                           189

Appendix: Principles of effective practice                             191
References                                                             193
Index                                                                  207

# ACKNOWLEDGMENTS

This second edition of *Working with Involuntary Clients* continues to be inspired by William Reid's work on task-centred casework and by Don Andrews and his colleagues' work on pro-social modelling. While they come from different perspectives, their publications have provided the background for a great deal of my own research and for much of the material contained in this book.

In writing the second edition I remain indebted to those people who assisted me with the first edition, in particular Michael Clanchy, Jan Mumford, Lloyd Owen, Colin Roberts and Rosemary Sheehan, as well as the many other colleagues, students and welfare professionals who provided me with case examples and who helped me develop the ideas and practices which are outlined in the book. Thanks also to Elizabeth Weiss from Allen & Unwin, who saw the potential of the book at the outset and has continued, with Alex Nahlous, to assist with this edition.

Finally, thank you Joan, David and Rebecca and Moo for believing in me and for your ongoing support.

*Note:* For seminars or videos on working with involuntary clients, Associate Professor Chris Trotter can be contacted on email chris.trotter@med.monash.edu.au

# 1 INTRODUCTION

How do you help someone who has no interest in being helped? What can you do with clients in the welfare or justice systems who are not motivated to change? How do you counsel someone who does not even recognise that they have a problem? How do you work with someone who has a totally different set of values from yourself? How can you help someone deal with their problems and at the same time exercise authority over them?

These are questions which workers with involuntary clients face on a daily basis. These workers are asked to help clients who have not chosen to be helped and who may be resistant or even openly antagonistic to the assistance they are offered; to help clients and at the same time collect information which may subsequently be used against them; to testify against clients in court and then to work with them in a helping relationship; and to work in a collaborative manner with clients, yet make authoritative decisions about their lives.

This book aims to help workers with involuntary clients come to terms with these issues.

# Who are involuntary clients?

An offender visits a probation officer; a child protection worker visits a mother following an anonymous report of child abuse; a drug user attends for drug treatment under the direction of a court order; a man who has abused his wife attends domestic violence counselling at the direction of a court; a psychiatric patient who is a danger to herself and others is directed to treatment as an alternative to hospitalisation; a young person living on the streets agrees to go to a refuge with his youth worker knowing that the alternative is for him to be taken to the police; or a child is placed in a children's home despite the protestations of the parents.

These are examples of involuntary clients. The clients (or recipients of welfare or legal services) in these examples can be described as involuntary because they have not chosen to receive the services they are being given. In fact, these clients might actively be opposed to receiving the service. They might believe that it is unnecessary and intrusive. The clients receive the service either because of a court order or under the threat of some other legal sanction. They are sometimes referred to as *mandated clients* (Rooney 1992; Ivanoff et al. 1994; De Jong and Berg 2001).

The clients in these examples are clearly involuntary. In many instances, however, the distinction between voluntary and involuntary clients is not so clear. In the following examples, the clients are not required by a court order—or even the threat of a court order—to receive services; however, their participation is motivated by pressures other than their own desire to address their problems: a mother whose child has been removed by child protection services seeks assistance from a family counselling agency to help get her child back; a drug user seeks rehabilitation counselling prior to a court appearance; an abusive man seeks anger management counselling in response to his partner's threats to leave; or a pregnant teenager visits a counselling agency at her parents' insistence. These clients are partly voluntary and partly involuntary.

Others who receive services are more obviously voluntary—for example, a student who seeks assistance from a student counsellor; a couple who seek relationship counselling; a parent who seeks assistance with children who are out of control; or an alcoholic who seeks assistance from a drug rehabilitation centre.

There may also be involuntary aspects of work with clients who choose to receive services, as well as voluntary aspects of work with court-ordered clients. For example, a student who seeks the assistance of a student counsellor might feel compelled to do so in order to pass her course, or a woman might attend marriage counselling as a result of pressure from her spouse. To give another example, a probationer might visit his probation officer on a voluntary basis in order to discuss problems in his personal relationships.

The distinction between voluntary and involuntary clients is therefore not always clear. It is perhaps best viewed on a continuum, with court-ordered clients towards one end, partially voluntary clients in the middle, and clients who seek services on a voluntary basis towards the other end.

This book is about work with clients who fall at the involuntary end of the continuum. Its particular focus is on work in the community with involuntary clients, carried out by probation officers (or community corrections officers) and child protection agencies. Few clients in these settings are voluntary, or even partially voluntary. Nevertheless, many of the practice principles discussed also apply to work with involuntary clients in institutions such as prisons, children's homes and psychiatric hospitals. In many cases, the principles are also relevant to clients who might be described as partially voluntary, or even voluntary.

# The dual role of workers with involuntary clients

For the most part, workers dealing with involuntary clients work in the welfare or legal systems for government departments or for agencies funded by government departments. They generally have two roles:

a legalistic or surveillance role; and a helping, therapeutic or problem-solving role.

A probation officer, for example, has a responsibility to ensure that a probationer carries out the requirements of the court order. The probation officer is required to take action if a client fails to report or fails to comply with some other condition of the probation. The probation officer might have to report to a court about the progress of the probationer or undertake a risk assessment, which will influence the level of supervision offered to the client. Simultaneously, the probation officer works toward the rehabilitation of the offender by assisting with problems which may be related to the offending behaviour.

Similarly, a child protection worker has the dual task of investigating levels of abuse and the risk of reabuse, taking action to protect a child and possibly taking measures leading to prosecution of a perpetrator of abuse; at the same time, they assist the family with the problems that may have led to the abuse.

Reconciling the legalistic and helping roles in work with involuntary clients can be a difficult task. It is difficult for a worker to fulfil a helping role with a probationer when they are also taking action to have a probation order cancelled. Similarly, it can be difficult to fulfil the legal role where a close helping relationship has developed between the worker and client. A child protection worker who has worked with a family on a voluntary basis for a period of time, for example, may find it difficult if they suddenly have to take action to remove a child.

Coming to terms with this dual role is one of the greatest challenges in work with involuntary clients. Often workers and organisations find it easier to focus on one of the roles to the exclusion of the other. There are examples of workers with involuntary clients who focus almost exclusively on the legalistic role, and other instances where they focus almost exclusively on the helping role (Thorpe 1994; Trotter 1996b, 2004).

This issue is addressed throughout the chapters of this book. The book aims to assist workers to achieve an appropriate balance between the two roles.

# Direct practice

The focus of this book is on *direct practice* with involuntary clients. It refers only incidentally to community development, policy development and management. It is about the direct day-to-day work with individuals and families carried out by probation officers and child protection workers.

As I said earlier, the practice principles discussed here are also relevant to others who work with involuntary clients—for example, workers in psychiatric clinics, drug counsellors, youth workers, school welfare staff, domestic violence counsellors, family support workers, family counsellors and those who work with the aged.

The terminology used to describe direct practice work in welfare and corrections settings has changed over the years. In the 1970s and 1980s, the term 'casework' was popular; however, terms such as 'direct practice' or 'clinical practice' are more popular today. Workers with involuntary clients are often described today as 'case managers' rather than 'caseworkers'. To some extent, this change in terminology reflects a change in the way the work is conceptualised and carried out. Case managers tend to have a service coordination role rather than a direct service or therapeutic role—although, as Di Gursansky and her colleagues (2003) point out, there is a great deal of ambiguity surrounding the term, and the practice of case management may be very different in different settings.

The definition of direct practice workers as case managers rather than caseworkers is seen by some writers as problematic (Markiewicz 1994; Ife 1997; McMahon 1998; Searing 2003). They maintain that government department staff are increasingly being given responsibility for case management and case planning, with problem-solving or therapeutic services being left to often under-funded voluntary organisations. They argue that clients are more and more likely to be managed rather than helped.

The following case example in the area of child protection illustrates one way of looking at the differences between case management, problem-solving or therapeutic work, and case planning. A case plan involving a direct practice worker is developed which specifies where and with whom an abused child is to live, how often and in what circumstances that child will have access with family members, and what welfare services will be offered to the child and family members.

Following the development of the case plan, the client or client family is case managed. This involves a case manager coordinating the various professionals involved and ensuring that the case plan is carried out. The case management might be undertaken by a worker involved in the case planning or by another worker. Individual problem-solving work with the client may then be done by another worker. This work might involve, for example, working on problems in the relationship between family members or helping a child to deal with difficulties at school.

Each of these functions—case planning, case management and problem-solving—can be viewed as part of the direct practice process. This book focuses on these three functions as a holistic endeavour, defining direct practice as incorporating each of them. Nevertheless, the framework for effective work with involuntary clients presented here is likely to be useful for those with responsibility for only part of the direct practice process—for example, where the worker has a role exclusively as a case manager or planner, or where the worker has responsibility for therapeutic or problem-solving interventions without a coordination and planning role.

## Sources of knowledge in work with involuntary clients

A wide range of *theories* exist which influence welfare work with involuntary clients, including psychoanalytic theory, ego psychology, systems theory, behaviourist theory, human development theory, labelling theory, feminist theory, critical theory, differential association and modelling theory.

Work with involuntary clients is also influenced by *practice models* originating from a range of theoretical frameworks—for example, task-centred, ecological systems, transactional analysis, solution-focused, cognitive behavioural, rational emotive, narrative, motivational interviewing and a number of different family therapy models.

In addition, work with involuntary clients is influenced by *research findings*. For example, workers might be aware of research which suggests that peer group influence can impact on young offenders (Akers 1994; Andrews and Bonta 2003), or that working with client goals is more likely to lead to positive outcomes than working towards goals set by the worker (Trotter 1995a, 2004).

In addition to theories, practice models and research findings, workers may be influenced in their day-to-day work by their own *values and beliefs*—for example, that siblings should remain together wherever possible; that women deserve more than they often get in family situations; that marijuana is harmless; that the legal system is unfair; that offenders should be treated more harshly; or that the nuclear family is the best environment in which to raise children.

Workers may also be influenced by particular *life experiences*, both professional and personal. A case example illustrates this point. A worker in probation confronted a client with what she saw as the reality of his life situation. She said that she believed the client was wasting his life and should be actively seeking work. The client committed suicide shortly afterwards. This experience left the worker very cautious about confrontation with clients.

Workers are also influenced by accumulated life experience, sometimes referred to as *practice wisdom*. A worker may have worked with young homeless people for many years. She may have found that she is able to relate to these young people better if she has supported the young person through a critical incident in which the young person is distressed—for example, following an argument with a family member. Her experience leads her to try to be available to other young people on such occasions in order to build her relationships with them.

*Organisational expectations and norms* can affect workers too. An organisation can have a culture which pressures individual workers to behave in a certain way. For example, in one organisation in which I worked the culture was to see clients as soon as possible even if they arrived without an appointment. This was viewed as respectful. In another organisation, the culture was to expect clients to make an appointment for another time. This was viewed as helping clients to be responsible.

There are therefore many sources of knowledge for work with involuntary clients. Workers often have difficulty identifying how the different sources guide their work. I have conducted many workshops for direct practice workers over the years, and have consistently been struck by the difficulties workers have in articulating the sources of knowledge on which they base their work. A number of research studies have raised the same problem (e.g. Carew 1979; Ryan et al. 1995; Scourfield 2002; Chaffin and Freidrich 2004). This hardly seems surprising given the maze of theories and models, values and beliefs, research findings and organisational expectations which inform every worker's practice.

In work with involuntary clients, where value differences between workers and clients are likely to be accentuated, where the use of authority places particular demands on workers, where client motivation levels are likely to be low and where the development of the casework relationship can be problematic, sorting through the conceptual maze of theory and practice can be even more difficult.

# Evidence-based practice

In an attempt to make some sense of this conceptual maze of theory and practice, this book outlines a framework for practice based on the research about what actually works. It presents an *evidence-based practice model*.

What is evidence-based practice? Many definitions have been offered over a long period of time. William Reid (1992:7), for example, refers to empirical practice (an alternative expression for evidence-based practice) as that which 'gives primacy to research-based theories and interventions'. He also suggests that empirical practice may involve practitioners carrying out single case study evaluations on their own clients.

Mark Chaffin and Bill Friedrich (2004:2) refer to evidence-based practice in child abuse services as 'the competent and high fidelity implementation of practices that have been demonstrated safe and effective usually in randomized control trials'—a rather complex description. However, they go on to refer to a more simple description: 'practice based on scientific knowledge about what works'.

Aron Shlonsky and Leonard Gibbs (2004:137) talk about the *evidence-based practice process*, which involves 'a well built practice question, an efficient search for best evidence, a critical appraisal of that evidence and action based on the interchange between client preferences, practice experience and the best evidence'. They point out, however, that some see it as 'anything, which can be done with clients which is linked to an empirical study' (2004:137).

The definition I favour—and the one which is utilised in this book—views evidence-based practice simply as *the use of research findings as a primary source of knowledge for practice.* This is not to say that research findings should be the only source of knowledge for practice, or that theories, values or organisational expectations, for example, are not important. It simply maintains that research findings should be viewed as a primary source of knowledge.

Evidence-based practice involves a worker having knowledge of research findings in relation to the various practices in their particular field. For example, a probation officer might make a decision about the type of community work placement to which a young offender should be referred, taking into account knowledge about studies of the impact of association with other offenders on community worksites (Trotter 1995b). A worker in child protection might be familiar with research which suggests that children are less likely to be removed from families if the worker focuses on specific and achievable client goals (Smokowski and Wodarski 1996; Trotter 2004). The worker might therefore choose to work with a client to find relief child care for a mother rather than immediately address concerns about her use of drugs. Or a worker might choose to refer a sexually abused client for a cognitive behavioural intervention rather than non-directive supportive therapy because of her knowledge of the effectiveness of cognitive behavioural interventions (Berliner 2004).

## Criticisms of evidence-based practice

There has been much discussion among academics and practitioners about the nature and value of evidence-based practice. Evidence-based practice has its passionate supporters and its passionate detractors (see Mullen and Steiner 2004 for detailed references). Critics of evidence-based practice often argue in favour of practice wisdom, intuition and more qualitative research which focuses on individual experience. So what are some of the specific criticisms of evidence-based practice?

It is argued that evidence is often not available, or if it is available workers don't have the time or expertise to gather the research evidence they need. Even when they do have time, the evidence usually applies to groups of clients and can't be applied to every individual—no one intervention will work for everyone. Others simply take the view that you can make statistics prove anything, and they are suspicious of research findings.

It is argued that evidence-based practice is reductionist because the focus is on measurable outcomes; factors which are not easily measured are ignored. Value-based objectives such as empowerment and social justice, or more individual objectives such as the development of self-esteem, are not pursued simply because they are not amenable to measurement.

For example, a problem-solving or mediation approach to family work might be successful in reducing family conflict. However, such an approach might maintain a patriarchal or even abusive family structure. The work undertaken with the family might therefore achieve one of the goals of the intervention—reduced conflict—but not another more value-based goal—for the family to interact in a more equal manner.

Critics also argue that an evidence-based approach leads to the notion that there is one best answer and that it downplays diversity. As well as ignoring the objectives which are hard to measure, it often ignores the unspoken objectives which underlie many programs. The complexity surrounding objectives in work with involuntary clients represents a major difficulty for evidence-based practice, and therefore warrants some discussion here.

For example, most evidence-based work in corrections rests on the assumption that the purpose of corrections programs is to reduce reoffending rates or to divert offenders from the prison system. Similarly, evidence-based work in child protection often rests on the assumption that the aim of child protection services is to enhance the safety of children and to help children to remain with their natural families. The primary aim of work in a mental health setting may be to help clients remain in the community.

However, in reality, workers work with a complex syndrome of sometimes competing objectives. An example from probation illustrates this. One objective for a probation officer may be to help clients to become more law abiding—in other words, to rehabilitate offenders. However, the probation officer also has an objective of supervising a court order. This could involve, for example, directing clients to community work where they are required to work with other offenders. It might thus mitigate against the achievement of the rehabilitation objective, given the potential contaminating effects of association with other offenders on community worksites (Trotter 1995b).

The probation officer may also be required to administer a punishment. The client, the courts, the community, and the probation officer may all see probation as involving in part a level of deprivation of the offender's liberty. Again, this may not be consistent with the rehabilitation objective. For example, some research suggests that low-risk offenders are likely to reoffend less if they receive minimal levels of supervision (Andrews and Bonta 2003); however, the need to offer a certain level of sanction in response to an offence might require a higher level of supervision.

The probation officer may have a number of other objectives—for example, working well within a team or achieving early promotion to a more senior position. Again, the pursuit of a rehabilitation objective can be inconsistent with achieving these aims. The team may have a more punitive orientation, and workers might be rewarded with promotion for fitting in with this punitive approach.

To change the example slightly, research suggests that high-risk offenders (unlike low-risk offenders) are likely to reoffend less if they receive higher levels of supervision (Andrews et al. 1990); however, this might conflict with the worker's objective of facilitating justice. Disadvantaged groups of offenders might effectively receive higher penalties (through higher levels of supervision) because they share risk characteristics such as homelessness and lack of family support. This results in higher penalties for social disadvantage—a clear injustice.

The complexity surrounding the purpose of work with involuntary clients is not limited to corrections. A child protection worker, for example, might aim to keep children with their families; however, she may also have an objective of avoiding negative publicity. The child protection worker might therefore be reluctant to leave a child with his natural family during an assessment period because of the fear of negative publicity if the child were further injured, even though the worker may be aware of research which suggests that alternative placement may not lead to better long-term outcomes for the child (Gough 1993).

In addition to the confusion at an individual worker level, there is often confusion about purpose at an organisational level. For example, there is some evidence that the actual intent behind at least some corrections programs is to punish rather than rehabilitate offenders, despite public expressions to the contrary (Trotter 1996b). There is also some evidence that, while the intention of child protection services may be to reduce abuse, some politicians, managers and child protection workers may be more concerned about possible media exposure. This can lead to a focus on risk assessment rather than on treatment to reduce the abuse (Farmer 1999). This confusion about objectives at an organisational level inevitably makes it more difficult for direct practice workers to be clear about their purpose.

In short, workers with involuntary clients have multiple objectives. These are sometimes hard to measure, and may not even be articulated by the workers themselves or by their organisations. Evidence-based practice, however, tends to focus on a narrow range of objectives, apparently ignoring many of these other objectives. And this is just one of the criticisms levelled at evidence-based practice. So why does this book present an evidence-based practice model?

## Advantages of evidence-based practice

Proponents of evidence-based practice argue that, in work with most involuntary clients, there is a presenting problem which leads the person to become a client. The problem may be offending, neglect or abuse, self-harming behaviour, violence within marriage, or one of many others. Evidence-based practice takes the view that it is important for this presenting problem to be reduced or alleviated.

Research about how such presenting problems have been dealt with in the past, and which approaches have worked best, can give workers knowledge to guide their practice and lead to improved outcomes—that is, to less offending, abuse, violence or self-harming behaviour. Improved outcomes may not apply in every case, but overall those who follow evidence-based practices are likely to have better outcomes.

For example, research in probation informs us that supervision which simply focuses on the development of the relationship between worker and client is not generally related to reduced client reoffending rates (Andrews and Bonta 2003; Trotter 1996a). On the other hand, a focus on reinforcing client's pro-social expressions and actions in probation supervision *is* associated with reduced reoffending (Andrews and Bonta 2003; Trotter 1996a).

An approach to supervision which is informed by knowledge of this research (an evidence-based approach) is more likely to lead to reduced reoffending. While probation supervision has objectives other than reduced offending, if reduced offending is in fact one of the objectives, it seems hard to justify an approach which does not make use of research about how best to achieve it.

Evidence-based research is indeed more likely to focus on specific outcome measures, such as client satisfaction with service, reoffending or further abuse, and to ignore objectives which are hard to measure, such as social justice, self-esteem or emotional well-being. It seems to me, however, that this represents an argument for developing ways of *measuring* social justice, self-esteem or emotional well-being (if these are program or worker objectives) in order to examine the extent to which interventions are achieving these objectives. The alternative seems to be to simply ignore whether or not programs or interventions are achieving what they set out to achieve—hardly an optimal approach.

Similarly, the argument that evidence-based practice is inappropriate because it focuses on limited objectives and does not address the often unspoken objectives of workers seems flawed. Again, this criticism is not so much an argument against evidence-based practice, but rather a case for individual workers and organisations to be clear about what it is that they are aiming to achieve—and an argument in favour of a wider body of research which examines different outcome measures. If, for example, the real aim of a correctional program is to punish or to satisfy a perceived community need to see justice done, then in order to assess the effectiveness of that program a clearer definition of purpose is needed. Evidence-based practice certainly encourages this.

There is no doubt that evidence-based practice does not supply all the answers. There are many areas of practice with involuntary clients where insufficient research has been done, or where research findings are so equivocal that they can contribute little to day-to-day practice. In many instances, however, research has been undertaken using program objectives which are consistent with at least some of the objectives pursued by workers and organisations. In these instances, use of this research can lead to better outcomes for clients (such as less offending or less abuse).

Certainly the argument about the time and expertise required from workers is a reasonable one. There is no doubt that evidence-based practice requires some effort on the part of the practitioner. Nevertheless, there are clear advantages for workers who use effective practices—satisfied workers and satisfied clients tend to go together (Trotter 2004).

Evidence-based practice involves workers being clear about what they are trying to achieve, and making use of research findings in their day-to-day work. It does not deny the existence of values or diversity or the complexity of purpose. In fact, it is argued throughout this book that a conscious focus on values and purpose is vital to effective work with involuntary clients. Evidence-based practice does not deny the importance of theory; on the contrary, theory is vital to guide research and explain research findings. Evidence-based practice simply recognises that research allows us to learn from past experiences, and should therefore be a primary factor in guiding our work.

# The purpose of this book

This book aims to present a framework for practice with involuntary clients which is based on research about what works, a framework which makes some sense of the multiple sources of knowledge which workers use on a day-to-day basis in their work with involuntary clients.

The book also aims to present this material in a way which is user friendly. As I have said, it does seem that workers have difficulty both articulating and utilising the various sources of knowledge about their work with involuntary clients, and my aim here is to present the material in such a way that it is readily translatable into the day-to-day work situation.

By influencing those who work with involuntary clients, I hope in turn to influence outcomes for those clients. I am hopeful that this book can contribute something to the lives of the offenders, the abused women and children and others who might receive services from its readers.

Two other texts focusing on involuntary clients were published in the 1990s, *Strategies for Work with Involuntary Clients* by Ronald Rooney (1992) and *Involuntary Clients in Social Work Practice* by Andre Ivanoff, Betty Blythe and Tony Tripodi (1994). This book is different from these books in several ways. Unlike the others, it presents a specific integrated intervention model for work with involuntary clients which has been developed from evidence-based research about what works, and which has been shown to be successful in the author's own research. The model presented here has a particular focus on role clarification and pro-social modelling, in contrast to the other books. This book also focuses on work undertaken with involuntary clients by workers with various academic backgrounds, rather than focusing specifically on social work practice.

# The structure of the book

Chapter 2 summarises the theories and research about what works and what doesn't in work with involuntary clients. It refers to my own research carried out with offenders, with abused children and their families and with family groups. Chapter 2 outlines the research basis for the following chapters and it is therefore central to the book. Nevertheless, the following chapters offer a summary of the research material so that each one can stand alone. This leads to some level of repetition; however, it will save the reader the trouble of having to refer regularly to Chapter 2 to understand the research context.

Chapter 3 discusses clarifying the role of the worker. It addresses the dual roles of helping and of social control, and the different perceptions of role from the point of view of senior managers, workers and clients. It also identifies role-related issues which might be discussed between workers and clients. Case examples are used in this and subsequent chapters to illustrate the practice principles. Where these are actual examples, the details have been changed so the clients cannot be recognised.

Chapter 4 presents a framework for dealing with situations where workers and clients have different values and goals. It presents a method of encouraging more pro-social values. It also considers how culture and gender impact on both client and worker values and goals.

Chapter 5 outlines a collaborative problem-solving process for work with involuntary clients, including a framework for case management, case planning and the use of community resources.

Chapter 6 examines the worker–client relationship and the place of empathy and other interpersonal skills, including self-disclosure and humour, in work with involuntary clients.

Chapter 7 proposes a method for working with family groups where one or more members of the family is an involuntary client.

The final chapter, Chapter 8, considers how workers might evaluate their own practice.

# 2 WHAT WORKS AND WHAT DOESN'T?

Do offenders offend less as a result of the work their probation officers do with them? Are children safer as a result of the work child protection workers do with families? Do drug users use drugs less as a result of casework intervention? Are mental health patients less likely to be readmitted to hospital if they have a worker to assist them? Do involuntary clients benefit from supervision, casework or case management? Researchers have been attempting to answer these questions for many years. In fact, research into the effectiveness of work with involuntary clients has a controversial history. The early studies were pessimistic.

One of the most well-known reviews of the effectiveness of casework was undertaken by Joel Fischer in 1973. This review of research looked at the effectiveness of casework services offered by qualified social workers in the United States in a variety of fields, including juvenile corrections, schools, families and the elderly. Each of the studies had a control group and considered outcome measures such as court appearances, teacher ratings of students' behaviour and family functioning. While the review did not specify which of the studies were undertaken with involuntary clients, an examination of the study samples suggests that more than half were involuntary (e.g. five of the eleven studies reviewed focused on delinquent or 'pre-delinquent' young people).

Fischer concluded that 'lack of effectiveness seems to be the rule rather than the exception' (1973:376). However, while he found that casework services overall were ineffective, he argued that this disguised the fact that some clients benefited from services and some deteriorated as a result of the services. In other words, it was not so much that casework services had no effect, but that they had both beneficial and harmful effects—casework services could be for 'better or worse'. For example, some offenders offended more and some offended less after they were given casework services.

This theme has run through the research about effectiveness ever since. Hundreds of studies have pointed to the idea that some things work and some things don't. There are some direct practice approaches which lead to better outcomes for most clients, whether voluntary or involuntary, and there are some approaches which fairly consistently lead to poorer outcomes (e.g. Reid 1997a; Andrews and Bonta 2003; Trotter 2004).

Obviously, the direct practice approach is only one of the factors influencing client outcomes. Outcomes are also influenced by clients' personal resources, by their willingness to change, the availability of family or other supports, and the availability of community resources—for example, employment opportunities. Nevertheless, the direct practice approach is one important factor influencing client outcomes.

The extent to which the skills of the worker influence client outcomes is difficult to assess. I conducted a study in the area of probation in Melbourne, Australia, which found that the worker's skill made a difference of somewhere between 20 and 70 per cent to client reoffending rates (Trotter 1996a). Probation officers who made use of the practices identified as effective in the research were half as likely to have clients who went to prison. Similar strong associations between the nature of corrections programs and reoffending are reported in a review by Don Andrews and Jim Bonta (2003).

As I have suggested already, the 'what works' issue is controversial. Some reviews of the research literature continue to suggest that nothing works, or at least that many direct practice approaches are ineffectual (Andrews and Bonta 2003; McDonald 2001). However, these arguments are falling from favour. The weight of evidence, as illustrated later in this chapter, suggests that direct practice with involuntary clients can be influential—it can lead to substantially improved outcomes; however, it can also lead to poorer outcomes.

This chapter outlines the direct practice approaches or skills which research suggests are related to positive outcomes. Effective programs or positive outcomes are defined in different ways in different studies. Effectiveness is defined in this book in terms of *improvement in specific outcome measures*. These outcome measures relate to the objectives of the program or intervention. For the most part, an effective program or intervention is one which leads to a reduced incidence of presenting problems, such as child abuse or offending, or perhaps to improvements in client satisfaction or worker assessment of progress. In most of the effectiveness studies reported in this chapter, the outcome measures are compared with a control group which has received an alternative intervention or no intervention.

The chapter is divided into discussions about approaches which have consistently been found to be effective with involuntary clients, approaches which have been found to be effective in some situations or about which the research is equivocal, and approaches which the research suggests are ineffective or harmful. An effective practice model is outlined. The relationship between this model and other theories and models is then discussed.

In many instances, it is unclear whether the research studies relate to voluntary or involuntary clients. In child protection and corrections, the clients are nearly always involuntary. However, as discussed in Chapter 1, in areas such as domestic violence, mental health and drug treatment, clients may be voluntary or involuntary. The focus of this chapter is therefore on studies of child protection and corrections clients with some references to studies with other client groups in fields such as drug abuse, domestic violence and mental health.

# Approaches that work

The research suggests that effective work with involuntary clients is characterised by clear, honest and frequent discussions about the role of the worker and the role of the client in the direct practice process; by the worker focusing on modelling and encouraging pro-social expressions and actions by the client; and by the use of a collaborative problem-solving approach which focuses on the client's definitions of problems and goals.

## Role clarification

Outcomes are improved for involuntary clients when workers focus on helping them to understand the role of the worker and the role of the client in the direct practice process. This involves ongoing discussions about issues such as authority and how it might be used, the dual role of the worker as helper and social controller, the aims and purpose of the intervention from both client's and worker's perspectives, as well as issues relating to confidentiality. In short, clarifying role is about the question: 'What are we here for?'

Don Andrews and his colleagues (1979) examined tapes of probation interviews in Canada and found that probationers were significantly less likely to reoffend if interviews were characterised by frequent discussions about the probation order, and by clarity about rules and sanctions and how they would be applied.

Lawrence Shulman (1991), in his study on child protection in Canada, found that 'clarifying the worker's purpose and role' and 'reaching for client feedback on purpose' were related to a number of outcome measures, including client views about worker helpfulness.

A British publication, *Child Protection—Messages from Research*, suggests on the basis of a number of studies that effective work in child protection is characterised by honesty on the part of the worker and clarity about 'what is happening and the options available' (HMSO 1995:46).

Lynn Videka Sherman (1988) undertook a meta-analysis of the effectiveness of social work practice in mental health. Meta-analysis provides an alternative method of reviewing evidence-based literature. It can be described as 'a method of aggregating and statistically analysing the findings of several studies' (Fischer 1990:297). While Videka Sherman did not specify the extent to which clients were voluntary or involuntary, part of her study did focus on chronically ill mental health patients, many of whom were in the system on an involuntary basis. Videka Sherman found that mental health clients had better outcomes if 'the intervention and the client's role are described clearly and discussed with the client before intervention begins' (Videka Sherman 1988:326).

Jones and Alcabes (1993), in their book *Client Socialisation: The Achilles Heel of the Helping Professions*, argue on the basis of a research review in the areas of child abuse, drug abuse and mental health that client socialisation is the key to effective work. They view client social-isation as helping the client to become a client, or teaching 'those needing help how to become clients' (Jones and Alcabes 1993:xiii). This process involves the worker and client agreeing on the problem to be addressed and the help-seeker learning the role of client before entering a treatment phase. The prospective client becomes a client only when they accept and understand how the worker can help and what is expected of the client in the process.

My own studies, in probation (Trotter 1996a) and in child protection (Trotter 2004), have also pointed very clearly to the value of role clar-ification. These studies are discussed later in this chapter.

It is certainly apparent that one of the key skills in work with involuntary clients is the skill of *clarifying role*. This is addressed in some detail in Chapter 3.

## Reinforcing and modelling pro-social values

Research on work with involuntary clients points to the importance of approaches which reinforce and promote pro-social values. Defining 'pro-social' is not a simple task. Defined narrowly, it refers to values and actions which are non-criminal. Defined more broadly, it refers to values or actions which might be construed as the opposite to criminal— in other words, actions and values which support and care for others. Examples might include non-violent interaction in domestic situations, equal personal relationships, caring for your children, trying to support yourself financially and not abusing drugs. 'Pro-social' refers to values of non-sexism, non-racism, openness and tolerance. Chapter 4 discusses the meaning of the term in more detail, and deals with some of the complexities and controversies relating to the pro-social concept— in particular, the perception that pro-social values may support the status quo.

Pro-social modelling and reinforcement, as defined in this book and elsewhere (Trotter 1997a), involve workers identifying and being clear about the values they wish to promote and purposefully encouraging those values through the use of praise and other rewards. They also involve appropriate modelling of the values the worker seeks to promote, and challenging anti-social or pro-criminal expressions and actions.

There is a considerable amount of research, going back many years, which suggests that the pro-social concept is related to improved outcomes with a range of involuntary clients. John Masters and his colleagues (1987) reviewed more than 70 studies undertaken with a wide range of client groups, some voluntary and some involuntary, which made use of the modelling and reinforcement of positive behaviours. Each of the programs studied had successful outcomes on the measures used. The authors point to studies where modelling and demonstrating desirable behaviours have proved effective in changing the behaviour of psychiatric patients, intellectually disabled clients, children with behaviour problems and school refusers.

David Gough (1993) reviewed 23 studies of child protection programs which offered intervention based on the use of social learning theory. These programs involved the 'identification of inappropriate interactions (between parents and children), the re-inforcement of positive interactions and ignoring of negative behaviour' (Gough 1993:125). Gough indicates that these approaches were among the best researched in his review and that they were 'effective in cases of physical abuse' (Gough 1993:9). Pro-social modelling and reinforcement have also been found to be effective in groupwork with aggressive children in an educational setting (Letendre 1999).

Jim Barber (1995), in a review of literature relating to work with drug users who are resistant to treatment, also points to the value of interventions which reward and reinforce positive non-drug using behaviours and which confront rationalisations. Barber refers to one study (Miller et al. 1974) which produced substantial declines in consumption among alcohol users when they were rewarded with token payments following zero blood/alcohol readings. Similarly, a meta-analysis relating to the treatment of drug abusers by Acierno et al. (1994) points to the value of reinforcement of abstinence and behaviours which compete with drug use.

More than ten studies in both juvenile and adult probation have pointed to the importance of modelling and reinforcing pro-social values. These are reviewed in Trotter (1990, 1995a). Two particular studies are outlined here.

Don Andrews et al. (1979) examined tapes of probation interviews in Canada and found that, when probation officers modelled and reinforced pro-social comments and actions and also made use of empathy and reflective listening practices, their clients offended significantly less often than the clients of other probation officers. Andrews and his colleagues argue that the reinforcement process was only effective when the probation officers also had good relationships with their clients, developed through the use of empathy and reflective listening.

I conducted a study in Australia (Trotter 1990) which found that volunteer probation officers who were more pro-social had clients who offended significantly less often in comparison with clients of probation officers who were less pro-social. This occurred regardless of the levels of empathy of the probation officers. The measure of pro-social was taken from the California Personality Inventory socialisation scale, previously known as a delinquency scale (Gough 1960).

These findings are largely replicated in a later Australian study (Trotter 1993) which found that pro-social officers were more likely to use pro-social modelling and reinforcement, and were more effective. The details of this study, and a more recent study looking at pro-social modelling in child protection, are outlined later in this chapter.

Finally, a more recent study in the United Kingdom implemented pro-social modelling and reinforcement among staff on community work sites and found significant reductions in pro-criminal attitudes and self-perceived problems among those who successfully completed community work (Rex and Gelsthorpe 2002). A meta-analysis by Craig Dowden and Don Andrews (2004) also found that effective modelling by corrections staff in a range of situations was strongly and significantly related to reduced reoffence rates by clients.

## Collaborative problem-solving

The research into work with both voluntary and involuntary clients points to the importance of working with a collaborative problem-solving approach. In fact, problem-solving approaches have gained wide acceptance in welfare circles, and many of the recent texts in social work and welfare outline models of collaborative problem-solving (e.g. Compton and Galaway 2005; Hepworth et al. 2002).

Problem-solving involves working with the client's definition of the problem, developing modest achievable goals which are the client's rather than the worker's (or at least collaboratively developed), and identifying strategies with the client to achieve the goals. Evidence in support of problem-solving approaches goes back many years (e.g. Reid and Hanrahan 1982; Rubin 1985; Sheldon 1987). Rubin (1985:474) comments in his review of effective casework practices that:

These forms of practice [problem-solving] were found to be successful with such diverse groups as mildly to moderately retarded adults, chronic schizophrenics in after care, young non-chronic psychiatric inpatients, women in public assistance and low-income children experiencing school problems.

The study I referred to earlier undertaken by Don Andrews et al. (1979) in probation in Canada found a significant correlation between the use of a collaborative problem-solving approach and reduced reoffending by probationers. Problem-solving practices by probation officers were measured by examining audiotapes of the probation interviews. My own work in probation in Australia also found a relationship between the use of collaborative problem-solving by probation officers (measured by an analysis of file notes) and reduced offending and reductions in problems reported by clients (Trotter 1993, 1996a). The value of problem-solving by staff working in corrections was again confirmed in a meta-analysis undertaken by Craig Dowden and Don Andrews (2004), who found that the use of problem-solving was significantly related to low offence rates.

Shulman, in his study in child protection, found a relationship between partialising client concerns (or specifically defining problems) and positive outcomes. Similarly, Smokowski and Wodarski (1996), in their review of evidence-based practice in child welfare, found support for this approach. My child protection study (Trotter 2004) also found a significant relationship between problem-solving practices by workers and improved outcomes. There is also support for these approaches in mental health (Jones and Alcabes 1993; Reid 1997b).

Further support for problem-solving in work with involuntary clients comes from studies of cognitive behavioural programs directed at both groups and individuals. Cognitive behavioural interventions commonly include a problem-solving component along with strategies to address distorted and unproductive thinking. In recent years, they have proved to be effective in work in corrections, child protection, mental health and treatment for addictions (Barber 2002; Corcoran 2002; Kolko 2002; Polkki et al. 2004; Wilson et al. 2005).

When dealing with involuntary clients, it can be inappropriate to work with the client's definition of the problem towards client goals. A sex offender, for example, might not define his offending behaviour as a problem, and his goal might be to avoid detection in the future. A schizophrenic client who is required to take medication might view the medication, rather than the anti-social behaviour which occurs when she fails to use it, as the problem.

Nevertheless, the research consistently points to the need to work with client definitions of problems and goals with both involuntary and voluntary clients. In fact, problem-solving approaches which work with clear definitions of problems in clients' terms and clear achievable goals have received so much support in the research over the years that they have almost become the social work and welfare method.

Problem-solving is discussed further in Chapter 5, which considers how a collaborative problem-solving approach can be developed in work with involuntary clients who are often resistant and frequently have different goals to the worker. Chapter 5 also considers some of the criticisms of problem-solving approaches.

## An integrated approach

Outlined below are summaries of two studies I have undertaken in Victoria, Australia, the first in probation (Trotter 1993, 1995a, 1996a) and the second in child protection (Trotter 2002, 2004). These studies form the basis for much of the material presented in this book. For more detailed discussion about the aims, methodology and outcomes of the studies, see Trotter (1996a, 2004).

The corrections study was based on the hypothesis that probation officers who make use of the skills of role clarification, pro-social modelling and reinforcement, collaborative problem-solving and empathy (discussed in the next section) will have clients who will be more likely to experience reductions in their problems and less likely to reoffend than clients of officers who don't make use of these principles.

A group of 30 probation officers was offered a training course in these skills. Twelve probation officers agreed to make use of the skills with their next ten clients. The remaining eighteen did not continue with the project for a number of practical reasons—for example, they left their positions or took extended leave. The study sample was selected using a systematic random method. It consisted of 104 clients of those probation officers who undertook the training and agreed to make use of the model. The sample also included a control group consisting of 157 clients selected from the same offices as the experimental group but with different probation officers. A sample of clients of those probation officers who withdrew from the project but continued in the probation service (105) was also followed up; however, the results for this group were very similar to the control group and are therefore not reported here.

Data were collected through a questionnaire administered to clients and an analysis of client files and police records. The study found the following:

- File notes suggested that probation officers who completed the training and agreed to use the model were significantly more likely to use the skills compared with probation officers in the control group. In other words, probation officers were more likely to use the principles after training.
- Clients receiving supervision from those probation officers who did the training and agreed to use the model (the experimental group) were significantly more likely to report that their problems were reduced during the period of probation than clients in the control group. In fact, almost twice the number of clients in this group, in comparison to the control group, reported that their problems relating to drug use were reduced.
- The reoffence rates for clients in the experimental group were significantly lower than for clients in the control group after one and four years. For example, the imprisonment rate after one year for clients in the experimental group was almost 50 per cent lower compared with clients in the control group. This is illustrated in Table 2.1.

**Table 2.1   Trotter study (1996a) offender imprisonment rates after one year and four years**

|  | Experimental group | Control group |
| --- | --- | --- |
| One year (p = 0.04) | 13/104 (12%) | 33/157 (21%) |
| Four years (p = 0.02) | 27/104 (26%) | 61/157 (39%) |

- The model was most effective with young, high-risk, violent and drug-using offenders.
- The use of pro-social modelling and reinforcement, as revealed in file notes, was consistently, strongly and significantly correlated with lower reoffending and imprisonment rates.
- The use of problem-solving was related to reduced reoffending, although it was most influential in improving compliance with the probation order (e.g. keeping appointments and special conditions).
- The use of role clarification was correlated with lower reoffending, but not at significant levels. This may be explained by the tendency of probation officers to discuss issues of role after the probation officer became aware of reoffending.
- Probation officer empathy, as measured by a psychological test and by comments in file notes, was not related to client reoffending or imprisonment rates. However, judgmental comments in files (e.g. no-hoper, lazy, liar) were related to increased reoffending even when client risk levels were taken into account. While officer empathy was not a factor in client reoffending, an extreme lack of it was.
- The results of the study could not be explained by intervening variables such as frequency of contact between workers and clients, client risk levels, or the experience or education of the probation officers.

The results of this study are persuasive, particularly given their consistency with the studies cited earlier and the replicatory nature of the study. The results confirm the importance of workers modelling and reinforcing clients' pro-social comments and actions, and the use of collaborative problem-solving. While the study is less persuasive in relation to role clarification, this seems to have been due to a particular intervening variable. The study does not support the value of empathy, although it does suggest that judgmental attitudes are related to poor outcomes. Empathy and other elements of the worker–client relationship are discussed in the next section.

The second study (Trotter 2004) was undertaken in child protection in the eastern region of Melbourne. The aim of the study was to consider the way in which child protection workers use the skills of role clarification, pro-social modelling, collaborative problem-solving and relationship skills such as empathy, humour, self-disclosure and optimism, and how the use of these skills relates to outcomes for clients.

In order to gather the data, research officers interviewed 50 child protection workers and 282 clients, and observed thirteen interviews between clients and workers. The outcome measures included:

- child protection workers' estimates of the progress of the families with whom they worked;
- the extent to which the clients were satisfied with the outcomes of the child protection intervention;
- how long the cases remained open; and
- whether or not a child or children were placed away from the family in a departmental facility (e.g. foster care) during the period of contact with the worker.

It was apparent from the study that the child protection workers often did not use the effective practice skills—a worrying trend which is also apparent in studies in probation (Dowden and Andrews 2004). Nevertheless, when the workers used the skills, the outcomes were much better than when they did not use them. Some of the more interesting findings include:

- The study supported the value of role-clarification skills. For example, when clients saw their worker as both a helper and investigator, those clients had good outcomes. Workers who talked about their dual roles as both helper and investigator and who were clear about their expectations also had clients with good outcomes.

- The study supported the value of pro-social modelling and reinforcement. For example, workers who modelled simple courtesies such as keeping appointments, being punctual and doing what they said they would do had clients with particularly good outcomes. In fact, this alone often made the difference between good and bad outcomes.
- The study supported the value of collaborative problem-solving. For example, workers who focused on their clients' view of their problems, who worked with their clients' goals, and who carried out some tasks themselves had clients with good outcomes.
- The study also supported the value of relationship skills. Workers who were optimistic, who listened to their clients and who were not afraid to use humour and self-disclosure had clients with good outcomes.

# Approaches that sometimes work

This section outlines approaches to work with involuntary clients which the research suggests work with some client groups and not others, or about which the research is more equivocal.

## The worker–client relationship

This relationship is defined by Compton and Galaway (2005) as including seven elements:

- concern for clients;
- commitment to and acceptance of obligations toward clients;
- acceptance of the client as a person (as distinct from their actions);
- expectation or belief that people can change;
- empathy or understanding of the client's feelings and point of view;
- genuineness and congruence (or openness and consistency); and

- appropriate use of authority and power.

Other writers offer similar definitions, although O'Connor, Wilson and Setterlund (2003) include self-determination. To some extent, the definition of the relationship is individual. In this book, the relationship is viewed as incorporating interpersonal skills, such as empathy and reflective listening, self-disclosure, use of humour and optimism. The issues of authority and power, confrontation, genuineness and confidentiality are dealt with as part of discussions about the pro-social approach and role clarification in Chapters 3 and 4.

So how do the various elements of the relationship relate to outcomes for involuntary clients?

## Empathy

Empathy can be defined as understanding the client's feelings and point of view. Reflective listening is effectively a practical manifestation of empathy. It is a counselling technique which involves responding specifically to the feelings and content of the client's expressions.

It has long been argued that empathy is an essential skill in effective helping (Truax et al. 1966; Carkhuff 1969). Most recent texts in direct practice in welfare settings discuss empathy as an important aspect of counselling or helping work (e.g. Compton and Galaway 2005; Hepworth et al. 2002).

The research support for the use of empathy in work with involuntary clients is, however, somewhat equivocal. Don Andrews et al. (1979) found that probation officers who scored high on a psychological test of empathy had clients who offended more often than probation officers who scored low on the empathy test. Similarly, probation officers who made use of reflective listening practices in taped interviews had clients who offended more often.

As discussed earlier in this chapter, however, Andrews and his team also found that if probation officers had high levels of empathy, made use of reflective listening practices and also made use of pro-social modelling and reinforcement, their clients offended less often. In other words, when probation officers were pro-social and also had good relationship skills, their clients did well. On the other hand, when probation officers were less pro-social and more pro-criminal (on psychological tests and in interviews), and also demonstrated high levels of empathy and reflective listening, the clients did not do well. In fact, they offended nearly twice as often as other clients in the study.

It seems that empathy set the conditions for change; however, the direction of that change was dependent on the pro-social attitudes and skills of the probation officer. It seems that the use of empathy in response to pro-criminal comments by probationers gave some kind of subtle permission or sanction for continuing that behaviour, with the result that further offending occurred.

My own work on the relative effectiveness of empathy and pro-social approaches in probation in Australia suggests a different conclusion in relation to empathy. In my study, volunteer and professional probation officers who had high levels of empathy did no better or worse than probation officers who had low levels of empathy. And pro-social officers with high levels of empathy did no better than pro-social officers with low empathy levels. These studies used psychological tests of empathy (Trotter 1990, 1993) and measurements of the use of empathy in file notes (Trotter 1993, 1995a, 1996a).

However, as mentioned earlier, the one finding that was significant in this study related to the use of judgmental comments. When workers made judgmental comments in file notes (e.g. lazy, no-hoper), clients offended more than other clients, even after risk levels were taken into account.

Some work has been done on the use of empathy with other groups of involuntary clients. Andre Ivanoff and his colleagues (1994) cite several studies undertaken with a range of involuntary clients which point to the potential of a genuine, empathic, helping relationship to be overwhelming and even aversive. William Nugent and Helene Halvorson (1995) also found in role-played interview simulations that inappropriate paraphrasing of client comments could elicit anger, anxiety and depression in clients. These authors favour an approach involving the provision of possible alternative interpretations of the client's expressions rather than simply reflecting what the client has said. Another study with adults with alcohol dependence found that non-directive reflective listening made no contribution to reduced drinking in contrast to motivational enhancement therapy which significantly reduced drinking practices (Selman et al. 2001).

On the other hand, Lawrence Shulman (1991) found a positive relationship between helping child protection clients to manage their feelings and client perceptions of the worker as caring. Helping clients to manage their feelings was defined as 'reaching inside of silences, putting the clients' feelings into words, displaying understanding of clients' feelings and sharing workers' feelings' (Shulman 1991:44). Caring workers, in turn, did better on a number of client outcome measures. They were viewed by clients as more helpful, their clients spent less days in care (away from their parents) and were less likely to go to court. Shulman's notion of helping clients to manage their feelings is broader than the concept of empathy and reflective listening. This might help to explain the different findings. This, by the way, is one of a number of references I have made to Shulman's child protection study, even though it was published in 1991. It is certainly one of the few studies that have examined the relationship between specific worker skills and client outcomes, and for this reason it remains relevant today.

In my child protection study (Trotter 2004), there was surprisingly little use of reflective listening practices in the interviews observed by the research officers. However, when clients felt that their worker understood their point of view, those clients did better on all of the outcome measures, including time to case closure and removal of children. Similarly, when we asked the clients to talk about the things they appreciated most about their workers, the thing commented on most often by clients was that 'my worker listened to me'. Further, as in the corrections study, when clients identified their workers as critical and judgmental, they did particularly badly on the outcome measures.

The research in relation to the value of empathy in work with involuntary clients seems somewhat confusing. There is little doubt that workers with involuntary clients need to be able to listen to and understand their clients' point of view in order to work with client goals and definitions of problems. Judgmental approaches seem to be most unhelpful. It may be important, however, that workers also make use of pro-social modelling and reinforcement to ensure that the impact of empathy is positive rather than negative.

## Humour

Humour is rarely addressed in the direct practice literature, although it has been argued that it is an important skill in the helping professions, including work with involuntary clients.

David Pollio (1995) argues that humour can be an appropriate tool for work with voluntary and involuntary clients. He distinguishes between humour as a conscious technique and situational humour. He suggests that humour that arises from the direct practice situation can be both helpful and harmful, while the telling of jokes is almost always inappropriate. Humour, Pollio suggests, can be used to break an impasse in the casework process and humanise situations. On the other hand, he points out that it can also be demeaning and cause the client to become angry. He encourages the use of humour in situations where the client can understand the humour, where it suits the style of the worker and where it is appropriate to the situation.

There is some research evidence that humour is an important skill for the helping professions. Daniel Eckstein and his colleagues (2003), for example, refer to research which suggests in relation to couple and family counselling that humour can help reduce stress or tension, unblock barriers to solving problems and move couples closer together.

There is also some evidence that it can be helpful in work with involuntary clients. Lawrence Shulman (1991), in his study in child protection, found that child protection workers who had a sense of humour (rated by their supervisors) were more likely to be viewed by their clients as helpful, skilful and trustworthy. Their clients also had fewer admissions to care and fewer court appearances. My child protection study (Trotter 2004) found that, when clients rated their worker as having a sense of humour, they were more than twice as likely to be satisfied with the outcome of the child protection intervention than if they rated the worker as not having a sense of humour. Craig Dowden and Don Andrews (2004) also identify worker humour in their meta-analysis as one of a number of relationship factors which relate to reduced offending rates.

Dinne Jacobs (2003) points to the value of humour among colleagues. She found that child protection workers who were rated as functioning well by their supervisors commonly gained support from their families and friends and their coworkers—support from coworkers was characterised by venting and humour.

There is clearly a need for more work in this area to tease out the nature of effective and ineffective humour. It does seem, however, that in the meantime workers with involuntary clients should not be afraid of the use of humour in their day-to-day work. It may help to humanise their work, reduce tension and facilitate the problem-solving process.

## Optimism

Optimism is tied up with concepts of hope, expectation and self-efficacy. Others have discussed the different connotations of these words and the different meanings which may be attached to the term 'optimism' (see Gillham and Reivich 2004). Suffice to say at this stage that if the worker believes the client can change and if the client believes the worker can help, it seems that outcomes will be better.

Martin Seligman reviewed some of the research in this area in his books *Learned Optimism* (1990) and *The Optimistic Child* (1995). He reported on a particular study conducted in a school in the United States which offered a program in optimistic thinking to depressed children. The children subsequently demonstrated long-term reductions in depression. Seligman (1995) also cites a number of studies which have used the notion of learned optimism to facilitate cognitive change and behaviour change in aggressive and violent boys.

Work by Bandura (1977) has pointed to the importance of self-efficacy—in other words, the belief people have that they will be able to perform or cope with new behaviours and achieve their goals—in general counselling situations. Most of Bandura's work is done with voluntary clients, with a focus on phobias; nonetheless, the principles seem to have more general applicability. Anne-Linda Furstenberg and Kathleen Rounds (1995), for example, discuss the applicability of self-efficacy to social work settings.

A study by Stuart Kirk and Gary Koeske (1995) in mental health found that newly hired case managers recruited to work with difficult mental health clients did better if they were 'optimistic' rather than 'realistic'. Case managers (direct practice workers) who had higher expectations and hopefulness generally than other colleagues enjoyed higher levels of job satisfaction and were less likely to quit their positions. The study unfortunately did not examine client outcomes, although an earlier study by Gottschalk (1973) found a relationship between levels of hope among clients in a mental health clinic and subsequent improvement in the clients' mental health. More recent research points to the value of optimism among recovering substance abusers (Majer et al. 2003), for successful community adjustment in mental health settings (Hodges et al. 2003) and as an important general quality in mental health social work (Ryan et al. 2004).

The value of optimism was also confirmed in my child protection study (Trotter 2004). Optimistic workers had clients with good outcomes. It was also apparent from the study that, when clients believed that their worker could help, those clients had good outcomes. In other words, not only was it helpful for the worker to believe in the client's capacity to change, but it was also helpful for the client to believe in the worker's capacity to help.

The concepts of hope, expectation, self-efficacy and optimism run through much of the helping literature. Pro-social modelling and re-inforcement, with their focus on positives, and problem-solving, with its focus on modest goals and short-term successes, are consistent with these concepts. On the other hand, the pro-social approach would suggest that worker optimism about the client's capacity to change needs to be balanced with a willingness by the worker to challenge pro-criminal or anti-social comments and actions.

## Self-disclosure

In workshops I have conducted for probation officers and child protection workers, participants have expressed very different views about the issue of self-disclosure. Some workers feel that any level of self-disclosure is inappropriate. Participants suggest that they are often asked questions like: 'How old are you?' or 'Do you have children?' Some respond that it is not the client's business. Others believe that giving some personal information about their own family and interests enhances the working relationship.

Again, there is not a lot of research on this subject in relation to involuntary clients. Researching this area is difficult because self-disclosure seems to be so dependent on the particular context of interviews. Dean Hepworth and his colleagues (2002), in a brief review of social work literature on self-disclosure, suggest that the results are so mixed that little can be concluded from them, although they do suggest that the cold, detached, distant therapist may be particularly unhelpful. On the other hand, they point to two studies which reported increased symptomatic behaviour in paranoid schizophrenics following personal self-disclosure by practitioners.

Lawrence Shulman's (1991) study in the area of child protection suggests, however, that some level of self-disclosure may be helpful. Shulman found that self-disclosure, along with sharing the worker's feelings, was positively related to client perceptions of worker helpfulness and client outcomes.

Shulman refers to the specific example of responding to the questions: 'How old are you?' and 'Do you have children?' and he suggests that, rather than dismissing the client in this situation, the question can be used to explore the roles of the worker and the client. Shulman argues that the question should be answered honestly and be followed by an exploration of the client's apprehensions about the worker's ability to understand what it is like for the client.

My child protection study also sheds some light on this issue (Trotter 2004). The clients generally did not see worker self-disclosure as being very important; however, when they indicated that their workers used some self-disclosure, the outcomes were good.

The extent to which self-disclosure is appropriate in work with involuntary clients is therefore uncertain. It seems to be heavily dependent on the particular context in which the work takes place. I raise it here because it is an issue which is frequently spoken about by both students and professional workers, and because it does appear to be a factor which may be related to client outcomes and worker effectiveness. Like the use of humour, it seems that workers with involuntary clients should not be afraid to make some use of self-disclosure in appropriate situations. The issue of self-disclosure, along with the other relationship factors, is discussed further in Chapter 6.

## Case planning, case management and the use of community resources

Involuntary clients in many cases are involved with a range of agencies and workers. For example, a family involved in child protection could simultaneously be working with a family support worker, a drug treatment worker, a domestic violence counsellor, a school welfare worker, a child psychologist, a probation officer, a housing worker, a psychiatrist, a mental health worker and a financial counsellor.

In the 1960s and 1970s, in many countries around the world, there was a move towards integrating welfare services so that families would receive a generic service from one, or at most a few, workers. In more recent times, however, specialisation has flourished and the situation described above, where members of one client family could find themselves interacting with many workers, is not uncommon.

Those who work with involuntary clients often have a role as case managers. In other words, as discussed in Chapter 1, the worker is required to refer clients to other services, ensure that the client attends those services and undertake an ongoing assessment of the extent to which the services are meeting the client's needs.

There has been much criticism in recent years of the case management concept. These criticisms have a common theme.

Interventions by specialist agencies and specialist workers can be symptom-focused rather than person-focused. In other words, specialist workers focus on clients' drug use, family relationships, accommodation or mental health rather than adopting a holistic perspective on a range of client issues. And if the specialist workers do in fact focus on a range of client issues—for example, accommodation, family and drug issues—then there is likely to be overlap and repetition, with many workers doing much the same thing.

Case management is criticised because of the difficulties involved in planning and decision-making when a large number of people are involved. A stark illustration of this problem is provided by the examples of high-profile child protection clients who have died in preventable circumstances despite the involvement of numbers of professional workers. The case of Victoria Climbie in the United Kingdom provides one example. For months, Victoria was 'bound hand and foot and left without food' prior to her murder, despite the fact that she was known to four social service departments, three housing departments, two hospitals and three child protection teams (Laming 2003).

Another criticism of case management relates to the difficulties involved in developing a consistent approach to the client. I have argued in this chapter that effective work with involuntary clients involves the worker utilising the key skills of role clarification, a pro-social approach and problem-solving. In situations where several workers are involved, the roles of those workers inevitably become harder to define, and the consistent application of these skills is likely to be more difficult.

There is some research support for the criticisms of case management. Steib and Blome (2004) found in a research study in the area of child welfare that caseworkers unfamiliar with effective interventions tend to make referrals to a plethora of different agencies resulting in the spending of millions of dollars without any real benefits. Another study in a mental health setting (Slawinski 2004) found that case managers who were employed to provide practical assistance to clients so that they could obtain services they needed in fact began to provide services of a therapeutic nature themselves, even though they were asked to follow an administrative case management model aimed at directing clients to appropriate services.

Don Andrews (2001) found that there was a direct relationship between the number of problems addressed in corrections interventions and the likelihood of reoffending. Interventions which addressed as many as six client issues (or criminogenic needs, as he defines them) saw much greater reductions in reoffending than interventions which addressed only one or a few issues—again, an argument in favour of a holistic approach.

The criticisms of case management also receive some support in our child protection study (Trotter 2004). Clients were often referred to three or four different agencies, and sometimes as many as ten; however, almost 20 per cent did not follow up the referrals. Clients were more positive about workers who they described as helpers and supporters rather than as case managers. The child protection workers indicated that they did not generally work closely with the agencies to whom they referred, and they were somewhat ambivalent about how successful the referrals were.

It certainly seems that, given the generic nature of the key skills for work with involuntary clients, outcomes might be improved by maximising continuity of service with individual workers rather than referral to specialised services. Nevertheless, workers dealing with involuntary clients continue to be required to work within case management systems. How can they work effectively when their clients are expected to receive services from multiple agencies or multiple workers?

Rubin (1985), in his review of the effectiveness of social work practice, comments that a common thread in effective programs with physically and mentally disabled clients was support for case management principles. Case managers followed up referrals, did case plans, made links with community resources and facilitated consistency in treatment.

Anne Fortune (1992) considers the role of case management in the context of inadequate resources and emphasises the advantages for clients of a coordinated approach. She points to a number of studies which suggest that casework outcomes are improved, for both voluntary and involuntary clients, when direct practice workers go beyond their 'comfortable' referral networks and when they have an understanding of bureaucratic procedures.

Di Gursansky and her colleagues (2003) point to key case management principles. They argue that case management should be designed around consumers' needs, be individualised and consumer driven, and offer choice to consumers. It should involve contracts; services should be accountable and provide quality measurement; and they should be timely, responsive and time-limited. They should also involve evaluation and advocacy. See Gursansky (2003) for more detail on issues relating to case management.

It certainly seems that a rigorous approach to case management which monitors the work done by other agencies, and which involves them in planning as suggested by Jack Rothman (1991), is likely to be more successful. This issue is discussed further in Chapter 5.

## Work with families

There is a body of research which suggests that work with families can·be effective in changing the behaviour of involuntary clients and in improving family functioning. This appears to be particularly so if the work with families is based on the principles of effective practice discussed in this chapter.

There is little doubt that family problems are related to a range of anti-social behaviours among young people (Hinton et al. 2003). There is also considerable evidence that young offenders, drug users, young people with mental health problems and other at-risk young people can benefit from family-based treatments.

Alexander and Parsons (1973) undertook a study with young offenders which aimed to examine the effectiveness of different forms of family intervention. While this study was done a long time ago, it provides an excellent illustration of the potential for work with involuntary clients to be both positive and negative. The study was undertaken with a group of minor 'delinquents'. These young people (aged thirteen to sixteen) had been arrested or detained by a juvenile court for offences such as running away, truancy, shoplifting, or possession of soft drugs. Families were randomly assigned to one of four treatment conditions.

One of the treatment conditions included a short-term behavioural family intervention program using modelling and reinforcement by therapists of clear family communication patterns, clear presentation of demands, and alternative solutions and negotiation of privileges. Use was also made of contingency contracting involving an exchange of tasks or favours between family members—in other words, the approach incorporated the principles of problem-solving and pro-social modelling and reinforcement.

The study compared three control groups with the treatment group: a client-centred family group, which focused on client and family feelings; a psychodynamic group sponsored by the Mormon Church with a focus on insight; and a group which received no treatment.

Reoffending rates after six to eighteen months were 50 per cent in the no-treatment group; 47 per cent in the client-centred group; 73 per cent in the psychodynamic group; and 26 per cent in the short-term family behavioural treatment group. In other words, the group which used an approach consistent with the principles of effective practice with involuntary clients had a reoffending rate of about half that of the control groups—even lower in comparison with the psychodynamic control group.

Subsequent studies using a similar approach (now referred to as functional family therapy), in some instances with more serious young offenders, found similar positive results with sizeable reductions in reoffending rates (Alexander et al. 1978; Barton et al. 1985; Gordon et al. 1988; Gordon and Arbuthnot 1990; Sexton and Alexander 2002).

A more recent review of research on functional family therapy (Sexton and Alexander 2002) suggests that, in addition to its impact on reoffending, this approach is effective with young people facing problems relating to substance abuse, mental health, maltreatment and neglect and sexual offences. Further, it maintains its benefits even after five years and also shows benefits for other family members, particularly younger siblings.

Similar positive outcomes have been seen with multi-systemic therapy. Multi-systemic therapy is an intensive intervention approach which targets all aspects of the family and young person's situation, including parent education, family therapy, interactions with outside agencies, peers, schooling and neighbourhood support. Again, the research points to significant improvements in problems related to school attendance, rearrest rates, drug use, maltreatment and rates of institutionalisation (Sexton and Alexander 2002; Perkins-Dock 2001).

There is research support for other family-based treatments with involuntary clients, including family behavioural therapy, parent training and brief strategic family therapy (Perkins-Dock 2001). There is also support for family-based interventions with mental health patients—for example, Lynn Videka Sherman (1988), in a meta-analysis of intervention methods with chronic mental health patients, describes a home visit-based family intervention model based on social learning theory and family education which resulted in a threefold reduction in hospitalisations for schizophrenic patients.

Positive outcomes have also been reported in relation to involving families in the treatment of drug and alcohol abuse. Barry Loneck (1995) points to the vital role that family members can play in encouraging people with alcohol and drug problems to accept treatment, particularly when those people are resistant to receiving help.

My own work (Trotter 2000, 2002), examining the effectiveness of collaborative family counselling (a problem-solving model) with a range of voluntary and involuntary clients, also suggests that the use of this approach with family groups is effective. This is consistent with earlier research on family problem-solving by William Reid (1985, 1992).

My study involved teaching the collaborative family counselling model (as outlined in Chapter 7) to a group of final-year social work students, and also to a group of professional human service workers. The students and the workers then made use of the model with eighteen client families in local welfare agencies in Melbourne, Australia. For the most part, these clients were either involuntary or partially voluntary. Clients, workers and students were then followed up after the completion of an average of eight counselling sessions.

Ninety-five per cent of the workers and students who participated in the study stated that they found the intervention to be successful. Ninety per cent of the clients indicated that their primary problem had improved by the end of treatment, and 100 per cent of the clients indicated that they benefited from the intervention.

This study did not involve control groups or long-term follow-up; nevertheless, it does suggest that family problem-solving skills can be learned relatively quickly and that workers and clients find the collaborative family counselling process helpful. It is consistent with the research evidence that, for many involuntary clients, work with families—particularly of a behaviourist or problem-solving nature— may be a preferable method.

## Short-term versus long-term intervention

In the first edition of *Working with Involuntary Clients*, I pointed to a number of studies which suggested that short-term focused interventions were often more successful than longer term interventions. For example, William Reid and Ann Shyne (1969) published a study nearly four decades ago which compared long- and short-term treatment in a child welfare setting. They concluded that, in terms of client satisfaction with service, short-term treatment was preferable. In 1984, Ray Thomlinson argued in a review of effective casework practice that structured time-limited interventions are at least as effective as less structured open-ended interventions. Similar findings were seen in Videka Sherman's (1988) meta-analysis with mentally ill clients.

William Reid (1997b), in a review of time-limited services, points to studies supporting the value of such services with adult probationers, the chronically mentally ill, and parents seeking reunification with children in foster care. He also points to several studies which suggest the value of specific extensions of service rather than open-ended treatment.

However, more recent studies have pointed to the value of longer term interventions. It seems clear that the longer clients remain in treatment for drug and alcohol addictions, the better the outcomes (Jones and Alcabes 1993; Lurigio 2000; Zhang et al. 2003; Moos and Moos 2003; Longshore, Turner and Fain 2005). In fact, Arthur Lurigio (2000:515) suggests that 'effective treatments must be long term and intensive recognising that most drug problems are chronic and relapsing and that most drug users need time to break through denial and to become motivated'. He goes on to say that ideally treatment should be between three and nine months in duration.

There is also some evidence that duration of treatment may be a factor in work with other clients in the welfare system. For example, James Luiselli and his colleagues (2000) found that time spent in home-based treatment of children with developmental disorder and autism was related to improved functioning of the children involved. Similarly, Schepker, Grabbe and Jahn (2003) found that longer stays (more than 55 days) were beneficial for children and adolescents in inpatient psychiatric treatment.

It seems, therefore, that the argument in favour of short-term treatment is becoming less persuasive. Certainly the structured short-term interventions offered in the early studies on task-centred work proved to be more effective than longer term, less-structured interventions. However, increases in the length of the more structured and effective services offered today may lead to still greater effectiveness.

The literature on the extent to which intensity or frequency (as opposed to duration) of treatment relates to outcomes is also equivocal. There is, as outlined in the next section, considerable support for providing more frequent and more intensive services to high-risk clients. Yet a study published by Donna Coviello and her colleagues (2001) found no differences in outcomes between a twelve-hour per week program and a six-hour per week program which offered an outpatient psycho-social treatment for drug dependence, even though both groups showed improvement in level of functioning and drug use after treatment.

At this stage, it seems to be difficult to determine the most appropriate frequency or duration of contact without discussing the specific client group and the nature of the particular intervention.

# Client factors

This book focuses on worker practices and characteristics, and how they relate to client outcomes in work with involuntary clients. It was pointed out earlier, however, that there are a number of other factors—including the characteristics of the client—which also influence client outcomes. By taking these factors into account, direct practice workers may be more effective. Two of these factors include the level of risk of the client and peer group influence. The issue of client motivation and its relationship to outcomes is also discussed in this section.

### Focus on high-risk clients

The profile of risk assessment in work with involuntary clients has increased greatly in the past decade. According to Gwen Robinson (2003:109), 'the rise of risk assessment in probation practice has been rapid—some might say meteoric'. One of the child abuse databases refers to more than 800 books and articles on risk assessment. Risk assessment is also prevalent in mental health—particularly forensic mental health—as well as in youth justice and domestic violence.

There are obvious reasons for focusing on high-risk clients. They are likely to have serious problems, to cause further harm to others and to make demands on resources. In addition, at least in the corrections area, there is evidence that high-risk offenders in particular benefit from supervision and other rehabilitation programs.

Don Andrews and Jim Bonta and their colleagues (1990, 2003) point to the importance of workers focusing on high-risk clients in work in corrections. High-risk clients are those who are assessed as likely to reoffend, whereas low-risk clients are assessed as unlikely to reoffend. It is argued that, while high-risk offenders are likely to benefit from human services, low-risk offenders may in fact be stigmatised by those services and become more criminal. They refer to this notion as the 'risk principle'.

Don Andrews and Jim Bonta (2003) refer to four studies which have looked at the relationship between the intensity of treatment and the risk levels of clients. In each of the studies, the low-risk offenders were more prone to commit further offences if they received intensive supervision and less prone to commit further offences if they received minimal levels of supervision. On the other hand, high-risk offenders were less prone to commit further offences if they received intensive supervision and more prone to commit further offences if they received minimal supervision. One of the studies cited by Andrews and Bonta (2003) actually found that the reoffence rates were no different between high-risk and low-risk offenders when both groups were offered intensive supervision.

This trend was also evident in a recent study conducted at Monash University in Melbourne, Australia (Trotter and Sheehan 2005), which found that high-risk women released from prison were less than half as likely to return to prison if they were offered intensive supervision on parole following their release.

It does seem pretty clear that it is best to reserve intensive interventions for high-risk offenders. Similarly, in areas such as child protection and mental health, the immediate risk of further serious child abuse, of suicide or of hospitalisation will no doubt always be used as an argument to focus on high-risk clients.

Alongside the increasing interest in the notion of risk, there has been considerable development of actuarial risk-assessment tools. These are prevalent in criminal justice, child protection and mental health. These tools require workers to work through a number of individual items, usually with tick boxes. This allows for a score to be calculated which classifies the risk level of the client. There is evidence from a number of studies, including several meta-analyses, which suggests that actuarial assessments are more effective than clinical judgment in terms of assessing risk (Andrews and Bonta 2003; Shlonsky and Wagner 2005; Schwalbe 2004).

Risk assessment has its problems, as discussed in Chapter 5. The profiles may be filled out incorrectly, the outcomes may be ignored and the risk levels may be used as a method of assigning punishments rather than human services or treatment. Nevertheless, used correctly, they represent a method by which client outcomes can be improved.

## Peer group association

In work with involuntary clients, association with an anti-social peer group can be a factor which leads to poorer outcomes. Paul Gendreau and his colleagues (1996), in a meta-analysis of factors which predict recidivism, found that criminal companions were more closely related to recidivism than any other factor—including criminal history, social achievements such as education and employment, and drug use.

Many studies have pointed to the influence of peers on anti-social behaviours of all sorts, including self-cutting (Yip, Ngan and Lam 2002), mental health of adolescents (Davis, Tang and Co. 2002), heroin use (Eaves 2004) and other substance abuse (Adams-Berger 2003), risk behaviours among abused adolescents (Perkins and Jones 2004) and school dropouts (Lee and Mui-Ling 2003).

Not only is peer group association a powerful factor in the day-to-day lives of many involuntary clients, but it can also be a factor within human service interventions. In a study I undertook in corrections (Trotter 1995b), I examined the relationship between reoffending rates of probationers and the nature of their community work placements. These placements involved working either alone or with other offenders on non-profit projects of some sort—for example, gardening or maintenance at schools, or assisting staff and participants in a sheltered workshop.

It was evident that offenders who were placed on community worksites with groups of other offenders were significantly more likely to reoffend. In fact, for offenders under the age of 21, the chance of them going to prison during the period of probation was three times greater if they were placed on a group worksite as opposed to an individual worksite. The differences could not be explained by the risk levels of the clients. The magnitude of these differences is surprising; however, similar results were found in a study conducted by Gil McIvor (1992) in Scotland.

The influence of peers on behaviour has long been known. Ronald Akers suggests that:

> Other than one's prior deviant behaviour the best single predictor of the onset, continuance or desistance of crime and delinquency is differential association with conforming or law violating peers ... Virtually every study that includes a peer association variable finds it to be significantly and, usually, most strongly related to delinquency, alcohol and drug abuse, adult crime and other forms of deviant behaviour. (Akers 1994:104)

It may, of course, be that those who are prone to anti-social behaviour are more inclined to mix with anti-social peers. Which comes first: the anti-social peers or the anti-social behaviour? My corrections study referred to above suggests that peer groups are an active negative influence—the negative peer group influence was apparent despite the fact that the community workers had no say in who they were placed with. This view is supported by Colin Roberts' (1993) review of corrections programs, in which he argues that the high reoffending rates of institutionalised offenders may be explained, at least in part, by the criminal subculture of prisons and the reinforcement of criminal attitudes.

Peer group association is certainly a factor which relates to the progress of many involuntary clients. And, as Don Andrews and Jim Bonta (2003) point out, interventions which target factors such as anti-social companions are likely to be more successful.

## Groupwork

This is not to say that there are not successful group programs with involuntary clients. There is, for example, considerable research support for the effectiveness of cognitive behavioural group programs for offenders (Wilson, Bouffard and Mackenzie 2005). There is also some support for group programs for violent men (e.g. Mullender 1996), for drug users (e.g. Milgram and Rubin 1992) and for psychiatric clients (e.g. Videka Sherman 1988). In fact, in recent years groupwork has become increasingly popular in corrections in both community and institutional settings. In the words of Maurice Vanstone (2004:191), groupwork has 'moved from a marginalized activity of a few enthusiasts to the centre of the effective practice project'.

The focus of this book is clearly on direct practice with individuals and families rather than groupwork, and the arguments for and against the use of groups are complex (e.g. Moore et al. 1997; Reid 1997b; Vanstone 2004). The research does suggest, however, that effective groupwork is likely to be characterised by similar practices to those referred to in this chapter. For example, Joan Ferguson (1983), in her meta-analysis of groupwork with offenders, found that groups were successful when they included pro-social modelling and reinforcement, problem-solving and an advocacy broker facility.

It does appear that, while groupwork is often effective, the unstructured mixing of involuntary clients has the potential to be problematic. The anti-social attitudes and actions which have led clients into the system may well be reinforced by programs which encourage association between people who have similar views, particularly if this association is not part of a program which makes use of effective practice principles.

## Motivation

One factor which is often raised by students and professional workers relates to clients' levels of motivation. Students and professional workers often comment that you cannot change someone who does not want to change, and that workers' energies may be wasted on unmotivated clients. Yet the issue is more complex than this.

Involuntary clients are for the most part motivated by a court order or the threat of some legal action. Given a choice, they would not be involved with the direct practice worker. Nevertheless, once they are involved in the client–worker relationship, they may be motivated to different degrees. Such motivation is, however, very hard to measure. A perpetrator of domestic violence might, for example, say that he wishes to change his violent behaviour towards his wife, or a drug user might say that he wishes to give up drugs. The behaviour of these clients, on the other hand, may not reflect this.

The complexity of the motivation issue is highlighted by studies in probation supervision which suggest that high-risk offenders—perhaps the ones least likely to be motivated to change—are most likely to benefit from supervision (Andrews and Bonta 2003). Lynn Videka Sherman (1988) found no association between voluntary and involuntary participation and outcomes among mental health clients. Another study found that people with alcohol and drug problems who were resistant to treatment could be encouraged to become involved by confrontation and encouragement from family members (Loneck 1995).

In contrast, Jones and Alcabes (1993) argue that, in child protection, readiness to change is important in terms of improved client outcomes. A study by Thomas O'Hare (1991) in mental health also supports this view. O'Hare considered 'readiness to change' in court-ordered and voluntary clients in mental health. He made use of a stages-of-change-scale involving four stages: pre-contemplation; contemplation; action; and maintenance. He found that voluntary clients were much more likely to express engagement in the change process, although many involuntary clients were also interested in changing. He suggests that 28 per cent of involuntary clients were at least at the contemplation stage, compared with 55 per cent of voluntary clients.

My child protection study sheds some light on this issue (Trotter 2004). When *workers* felt that their clients were motivated towards change, those clients did better on the outcome measures. However, when the *clients* said they were motivated to change, it made no difference to the outcomes. On the other hand, when the clients said that they expected that their worker would help, the outcomes were clearly better. Further, when the clients indicated that their worker believed that they could change, the outcomes were also better. In other words, when the worker saw the client's potential and when the client saw the worker's potential to help, the outcomes were good.

The issue of client motivation is therefore a complex one. Levels of client motivation are difficult to separate from the interaction which exists between worker and client. As Beulah Compton and Burt

Galaway (2005) argue, clients are much more likely to be motivated if they are pursuing their own important goals rather than someone else's. Certainly the notion that involuntary clients are unmotivated and therefore cannot change is an oversimplification.

# Approaches that don't work

While the research strongly suggests that some approaches to work with involuntary clients are indeed effective, it is apparent that direct practice with involuntary clients has the capacity to be both helpful and harmful.

Approaches which blame, punish and judge clients in the hope that their behaviour will change seem doomed to failure—whether they are used with young offenders, parents who have abused their children, perpetrators of domestic violence or any other involuntary clients. Of course, there are sometimes occasions when the inevitable consequences of clients' actions need to be pointed out to them, or when pro-criminal or anti-social actions and comments should be challenged. Indeed, I argue strongly in Chapter 4 that they should be. However, blaming and punishment—particularly where they are not accompanied by attempts to address client problems or to reinforce positives—do not work. The poor outcomes for day-in-gaol programs (in which young offenders are placed in gaol for a day) and similar programs which have attempted to scare young offenders into going straight provide a good example of this (Lipsey 1991; Gendreau 1996; Andrews and Bonta 2003). Similarly, child protection programs have found that the threat of imprisonment or removing children is not necessarily effective in changing parental behaviour (Gough 1993).

Interventions which focus on insight alone, or solely on the relationship, and do not include problem-solving or pro-social dimensions, have limited support in work with involuntary clients (Trotter 1991, 1996a; Gough 1993; Selman et al. 2001). Interventions which focus on worker goals rather than achievable client goals or goals agreed on between worker and client do not seem to work either (Thomlinson 1984; Rubin 1985; Jones and Alcabes 1993; Trotter 2004).

Poor outcomes have followed in situations where there is uncertainty on the part of the client, or the worker, about the purpose of the intervention, about the role of the worker as social controller or helper, and about how authority will be used (Andrews et al. 1979; Videka Sherman 1988; Shulman 1991; Jones and Alcabes 1993; Polkki et al.; Trotter 2004). Similarly, a lack of clarity about what is expected of the client and what is negotiable and what is not negotiable is related to poor outcomes (Dowden and Andrews 2004; Trotter 2004).

A pessimistic view about the client's capacity to change, a focus on what clients are doing wrong, and a reluctance to encourage and reward positive behaviours are all related to poorer outcomes for involuntary clients (Andrews et al. 1979; Masters et al. 1987; Shulman 1991; Trotter 1996a, 2004).

Poor modelling by the worker, particularly in terms of unreliability, lateness and poor follow-through on tasks, is related to poor outcomes (Dowden and Andrews 2004; Trotter 2004).

A focus on the individual and viewing the individual as the problem rather than focusing on the client in the family and social context also seems to be related to poorer outcomes for involuntary clients (Rubin 1985; Fortune 1992; Trotter 2004).

# An evidence-based practice model

The following chapters of this book outline a practice model based on research about what works and on the model which was developed in my own work in corrections and child protection (Trotter 1991, 1996a, 2004). It focuses particularly on role clarification, pro-social modelling and reinforcement, collaborative problem-solving and building relationships.

The practice model is often described as the *pro-social model*. Sally Cherry (2005), in a new book on pro-social modelling, uses the term pro-social practice. While these terms only describe one aspect of the model, the many probation officers and child protection workers who have undertaken seminars and training in the model around the world have adopted this terminology. In this book, I am therefore using the term 'pro-social practice' to refer to the integrated model as a whole. In using the terms 'pro-social approach', or 'pro-social modelling and reinforcement', I am referring to the specific practices of pro-social modelling, pro-social reinforcement and challenging pro-criminal or anti-social comments and actions.

Other practice principles which the research suggests are related to effective work with involuntary clients are incorporated into the practice model, either directly or through the use of case examples. In particular, the model incorporates the use of self-disclosure, confrontation and humour, case management principles and making referrals. While this book presents an evidence-based practice model, reference is also made to other sources of knowledge referred to in Chapter 1, such as values and organisational expectations.

The book therefore attempts to incorporate a range of skills and approaches into an integrated practice model. There is some evidence from meta-analytic reviews that multi-component approaches such as this are more effective (Andrews et al. 1990; Reid 1997a; Andrews and Bonta 2003). In other words, more effective approaches involve the use of a number of different approaches, rather than relying on one single theory such as behaviourist theory or psychoanalytic theory.

It will have become clear that much of my own work on the development of this practice model has been in correctional and child protection settings. I have argued, however, that the principles underlying the model apply generally in work with involuntary clients.

# Research evidence, theory and other practice models

I suggested in Chapter 1 that theories help to guide research and explain research findings. One would therefore expect an effective practice model to be both supported by research findings and consistent with one or more theoretical perspectives. In other words, a practice model should not only work, it should be clear *why* it works.

It is not the aim in this book to examine theories in any detail. The practice model presented is derived primarily from research findings. Nevertheless, some brief discussion about the relationship between this practice model and some of the more popular theories and practice models is appropriate.

## Ecological systems theory

Systems theory points to the interrelatedness of people and different events. The term 'ecological systems theory' uses a biological metaphor to illustrate the sometimes dramatic impact that intervening in one system may have on other systems.

Ecological systems theory points to the sometimes unexpected impacts that casework interventions might have. For example, a worker might facilitate reading classes for a mature-aged illiterate client. The newly acquired reading skill might impact on a spouse who feels less needed. This might in turn threaten a marital relationship which has been sustained by dependency. In turn, this might impact on the client's relationships with her children, who become involved somehow in the failing relationship. This might then impact on grandchildren who are close to the grandparents, and so on.

Systems theory also recognises the importance of roles which are ascribed to individuals and groups—for example, roles as parents or children, as women or men, or as worker or client. Systems theory highlights the importance of being aware of roles in work with clients.

Systems theory underlies the practice model presented in this book. Pro-social practice highlights the importance of understanding the client's situation in terms of the wider environment. It also highlights the importance of clarity about roles and the difficulties caseworkers may experience when they, or their clients, are confused about role expectations. The reader is referred to Germain and Gitterman (1996) or Kerson (2002) for a detailed description of a systems approach to direct practice.

## Behaviourist theory and cognitive behavioural treatments

Behaviourist theory, along with social learning theory, suggests—among other things—that anti-social behaviour may be developed as a result of association with anti-social peers, by exposure to anti-social role models and by reinforcement and rewarding of anti-social behaviour. On the other hand, pro-social behaviour may be developed through association with pro-social peers, exposure to pro-social role models and by reinforcing and rewarding pro-social behaviour (Akers 1994; Andrews and Bonta 2003).

Behaviour theory is therefore central to, and provides an explanation for, the positive research findings associated with the pro-social approach. Behaviourist theory is discussed further in Chapter 4.

Cognitive theory, unlike behaviourist theory, recognises that learning processes are influenced by thoughts and feelings. Cognitive therapy, rather than concentrating on behaviours, focuses on thought patterns and changing distorted thinking. While the pro-social approach is primarily behaviourist, problem-solving, role clarification and relationship skills focus on cognitive change as well as behaviour change. The practice model, as it is presented in this book, encourages clients to change anti-social thinking as well as anti-social behaviours. It therefore has something in common with cognitive therapies.

For more detail on cognitive behavioural approaches the reader is referred to Hepworth, Rooney and Larson (2002), Wilson, Bouffard and Mackenzie (2005) or Grant (2004).

## Feminist theory

While there are a number of different feminist approaches, feminist writers such as Jan Fook (1993, 2002) and Lena Dominelli (2002) suggest that there are some common themes in a feminist approach

57

to social work, including work with involuntary clients. In particular, feminist practice focuses on the way in which patriarchal systems disadvantage women through sex role stereotyping and devaluing of women's experience. Feminist approaches highlight the importance of helping women to understand their situation from a gender perspective.

Lena Dominelli (2002:7) defines feminist social work as 'a form of social work that takes women's experience of the world as a starting point of its analysis and by focusing on the links between a woman's position in society and her individual predicament, responds to her specific needs, creates egalitarian relations in "client" worker interactions and addresses structural inequalities'. While her focus is on social work, she does refer extensively in her book to work with involuntary clients, including children and families and offenders. She argues, for example, that working with offenders from a feminist perspective involves an acknowledgment of the importance of rehabilitation, of the punishment fitting the crime and of the 'eradication of discrimination against white women and black people' (Dominelli 2002:157). She argues that it is necessary to understand the impact of masculinity and power relations on men's offending behaviour, and to address this issue in a systematic manner.

Jan Fook (1986, 1993) suggests a number of specific strategies and techniques which are relevant to feminist casework. These include more equal interviewing settings (e.g. in the client's home); gathering of information in the assessment stage which relates to gender role expectations and labelling; the use of therapeutic techniques such as empathy and critical questioning to identify socially conditioned assumptions; the use of equal and non-authoritarian relationship styles; and providing information and advocating on behalf of the client. Fook also refers to the value of modelling as an educational process.

The practice model presented in this book has elements in common with feminist practice. For example, its focus—like that of feminist practice—is on equal relationships and on positives and strengths rather than on negatives or client shortcomings.

The pro-social approach, in recognising the importance of values in the direct practice process, also provides a framework for the practical implementation of a feminist approach. The worker can identify and reinforce comments and actions which acknowledge feminist interpretations of events. The worker can model behaviour which is consistent with feminist values. Through the problem-solving process, the worker can also encourage clients to explore feminist interpretations of problems.

## Critical theory

Critical theory has much in common with feminist theory. It is based on a premise that social problems are in large part socially constructed. It accepts some of the traditional Marxist views that client problems are often related to socio-economic or structural factors such as class and role expectations, inequality, poverty, poor housing, unemployment and inadequate social security systems. It encourages consciousness-raising, advocacy and social action.

Critical theory also points to the role that recent political and economic activity has played in the escalation of social problems, in particular globalisation, economic rationalism, managerialism, corporatism, privatisation and the accompanying erosion of public services (Morley 2003). Critical theory emphasises that the oppression of many groups in society, including the involuntary clients discussed in this book, is sustained by adherence to the dominant discourses of economic rationalism and corporatisation. Critical theory is concerned about the oppression of groups on the basis of race, gender, age, disability, illness and poverty.

Critical theory acknowledges that knowledge is socially constructed, and meanings are contextual. In other words, how we understand phenomena such as crime or child abuse is grounded in a time and a place. Critical theory accepts the postmodern perspective of the relativistic and subjective nature of the world, and it asserts that how we view the world shapes how we respond to it (Spratt and Houston 1999).

What are the implications of critical theory for day-to-day work with involuntary clients? Christine Morley (2003) points to some of these in an article about critical reflection workshops she undertook with workers from a human service agency in Australia. Following the workshops, the workers became more aware of the language they used, 'consciously decided not to buy into discourses which were devaluing' and 'put boundaries around their availability relating to excessive workloads, unpaid overtime and working during lunch breaks' (Morley 2004:302).

Spratt and Houston (1999) refer, in an article about developing critical social work in child protection, to a number of implications for practice. They suggest that child protection workers can see their work from a number of ideologies—for example, a penal ideology which views child abuse as a deliberate act, a blaming, 'protect your back' ideology, a medical ideology which views child abuse as a disease, a bureaucratic or a humanist ideology. They suggest that the critical practitioner would take as a starting point a humanist ideology 'that structural processes produce inequalities that generate (unfortunate) responses to these conditions which are best explained by social context rather than individual pathology' (Spratt and Houston 1999:5). In other words, they need resources not therapy.

In practical terms, this involves constructing the client's situation in terms of needs/problems rather than risk—focusing on family group conferencing, for example, rather than the more impersonal case conference, and providing practical help and supports rather than therapy. Finally, rather than focus on procedures, the worker might 'reflect on the complexities of the case'.

The intervention model presented in this book is not a critical practice model. Nevertheless, some aspects of the model are consistent with critical theory. For example, workers are encouraged to think about the sources of knowledge which inform their practice. They are encouraged to think about what is pro-social and what isn't, and to think about what client actions and responses they encourage and discourage. The dangers of imposing the workers' and the organis-ation's views on clients are highlighted. The model involves seeing clients in their social context, taking a holistic approach to their problems, and encouraging clients to define problems from their own perspective. It is clearly a non-blaming intervention model.

## Task-centred practice

William Reid and his colleagues began developing task-centred casework many years ago (Reid and Epstein 1972), and a lot has been written about it since this time (e.g. Doel and Marsh 1992; Reid 1992; Marsh 2004). Task-centred casework is a problem-solving model for work with both voluntary and involuntary clients. It focuses particularly on the development of tasks to address problems.

Task-centred casework has many similarities with the practice model presented in this book. In particular, the problem-solving and the family problem-solving chapters owe much to the work of William Reid. This book does, however, adapt the task-centred model particularly to work with involuntary clients. The model presented here also, unlike task-centred approaches, focuses particularly on role clarification and the pro-social approach.

## Strengths-based, solution-focused and narrative approaches

Strengths-based work involves focusing on clients' strengths rather than their deficits. It is based on the belief that people learn more and progress better if their workers resist focusing on pathology and instead focus on the things that their clients do well and on their achievements. It is based on the belief that even the most problem-saturated person has inner resources which can help them develop (Saleebey 2001).

Strengths-based work is a key part of solution-focused counselling. Solution-focused counselling offers particular techniques for focusing on strengths. For example, it asks workers to focus on times when the problem was not present—to search for exceptions to the rule. It refers to the notion of 'if it works do it more', and it encourages clients to picture the way things *could be*, rather than the way they *are* (Baker and Steiner 1995).

Strengths-based work is also a key part of narrative therapy which focuses on helping clients to re-author their unhelpful life stories into more productive and strengths-based life stories (White and Epston 1989).

Strengths-based work also ties into the notion of developing client resilience—in other words, developing the capacity of clients to thrive despite a high degree of stress and a poor environment. It involves fostering clients' individual capacity to handle negative experiences by tapping into their individual resources and tapping into supports within their families or wider networks (Gilligan 2001; Allison et al. 2003).

The intervention model outlined in this book has much in common with these strengths-based approaches. Pro-social practice is a strengths-based approach which focuses on optimism, client goals and solutions. It is, however, unlike solution-focused approaches in its focus on research findings, its focus on identifying and exploring problems, its specific promotion of pro-social actions and expressions, and its focus on confrontation.

Pro-social practice also has much in common with narrative work. Problem-solving involves examining a client's 'real' stories from the client's perspective, and it involves helping the client to see different possibilities—although it differs from narrative approaches in that it encourages a focus on risk-related issues or problems and uses a specific structure to work through problems.

## Motivational interviewing

Motivational interviewing was initially developed as a therapeutic approach to address addictive behaviours. It focuses on understanding the client's point of view, developing goals, accepting the client's autonomy, working with the client's definition of the problem and simultaneously persuading the client towards change. It also makes use of the notion of building confidence that change is possible and differential reinforcement of client comments (Hohman 1998; Moyers and Rollnick 2002).

Motivational interviewing has much in common with the model developed in this book. It varies from motivational interviewing, however, as it is more specifically targeted towards statutory clients, it is more likely to focus on situations where the worker and the client have different views about the goals of the intervention, and it focuses more on developing intervention strategies rather than simply fostering motivation.

## Other approaches

There are many other theories and models which influence direct practice with involuntary clients. I have attempted simply to highlight a few of the similarities and differences between the evidence-based model presented in this book and some of the more popular theories and models which are often used in work with involuntary clients.

# Summary

The research on work with involuntary clients suggests that some things work better than others. There are certain generic practice principles which seem to be effective with most, if not all, groups of involuntary clients. These include: accurate role clarification; working with problems and goals as they are defined by the client; and modelling and reinforcing pro-social values.

There are a number of other approaches or practice skills which seem to relate to positive outcomes; however, in some instances the research is equivocal about them and in other instances they seem to be effective with only some groups of involuntary clients. These include: the client–worker relationship; case planning, case management and the use of community resources; work with families; and short-term interventions. There are also a number of client factors which relate to outcomes such as risk levels, peer group association and client motivation.

There are some approaches which the research suggests are generally related to minimal impact or poorer outcomes. These include: approaches which seek merely to blame or punish clients; approaches which focus exclusively on insight or the client–worker relationship; working with problems and goals defined by the worker alone; confusion and dishonesty on the part of the worker about role and how authority will be used; pessimism and negative focus; and failing to see the client in a family and social context.

A practice model for work with involuntary clients has been presented in this chapter, and some comments made about how this model relates to other theories and models. The following chapters outline the practice model in more detail.

# 3 ROLE CLARIFICATION

What are we here for? What do we hope to get out of this? What do we have to do? What do we have a choice about?

The research referred to in Chapter 2 suggests that clarity about these issues on the part of both worker and client is likely to be related to better outcomes for involuntary clients. The research suggests that role clarification should be viewed as one of the key skills in work with involuntary clients (Shulman 1991; Jones and Alcabes 1993; Andrews and Bonta 2003; Trotter 2004).

Clarification of role involves workers helping their clients to understand the nature of the direct practice process. It involves more than simply explaining the conditions of a court order or the mandate under which the worker operates. It is about exploring with clients the purpose of the intervention—what the worker and client each hope to achieve.

Clarification of role is an ongoing process. It occurs at the beginning of work with involuntary clients when basic details about legal responsibilities are usually discussed. It continues throughout the intervention process as worker and client explore the purpose of their time together. An explanation of role might take a few minutes, but ongoing exploration of role and continuing endeavours by the worker to help the client understand their own role and that of the worker might take many hours over a number of interviews.

Clarification of role occurs simultaneously with other aspects of the direct practice process. While exploring clients' perceptions of the role of the worker with them, the worker may the same time be reinforcing pro-social comments, working through the problem-solving process and making use of relationship skills such as empathy or optimism.

In seminars I have conducted with child protection workers, probation officers, school welfare workers and others who work with involuntary clients, workers have consistently referred to certain role-related issues which they believe should be discussed and explored with clients. These include: the dual (social control/welfare) role of the worker; what is negotiable and not negotiable, and how the worker's authority might be used; the client's expectations of the worker; confidentiality and who has a right to information; the nature of the professional relationship and what this means in terms of how the worker and client interact; the role of the worker as case manager, case planner or caseworker; the client's expectations of the casework process; the expectations the worker's employing organisation places on the worker and the client; and the theoretical approach the worker uses as a basis for their work.

Clarification of role involves the worker coming to terms with these issues and also helping clients to come to terms with them. The worker will often feel uncertainty about these issues, and the worker's views will often change as a result of different experiences. An effective worker, however, thinks through these issues and devotes time to discussing them with clients.

What is the nature of the role-related issues which workers might explore with involuntary clients?

# Dual role: Social control and helping

Chapter 1 highlighted the uncertainty workers often feel about the welfare versus social control (legalistic) dilemma. Is the primary purpose of work with involuntary clients to administer a court order and to investigate anti-social behaviour, or is it to help clients with problems? The answer to this question is rarely clear cut. In fact, workers generally move between helping and legalistic roles at different stages of the direct practice process—even at different stages of an interview.

There are instances when workers with involuntary clients adopt a strongly legalistic focus. For example, a worker might be interviewing a father who has abused his child with a view to removing the child if he appears to be in danger of being injured again. The worker must collect detailed information about the circumstances of the father and the child to make an assessment of the child's immediate safety.

In this situation, the worker may feel that it is misleading to the client to suggest that they have a helping or problem-solving role. For example, the child protection worker, by working through issues or problems, could lead the client to divulge information which could result in subsequent removal of the child. The worker might feel that the use of a welfare or problem-solving approach could give the client a sense of having been misled or trapped.

In other instances, the worker might adopt a less legalistic and more welfare-oriented or problem-solving approach. In these instances, the more legalistic aspects of the work may be difficult. A child protection worker, after a number of visits, may feel that she is progressing well with a mother who has neglected her child. The worker may have worked through a number of problems and developed a close working relationship with the mother and her child, even though there continue to be serious concerns about the mother's parenting practices. The worker might feel in this instance that discussion about legalistic issues (e.g. the possible need for a return to court) would interfere with the working relationship.

This dilemma exists across the range of involuntary clients. For example, a homeless youth might be befriended by an outreach youth worker. The youth worker might be concerned about the young person's excessive drug use and feel it is necessary to report the matter to the police or child protection authorities. The youth worker might focus immediately on their legalistic role and feel that discussing their role as a helper in these circumstances is misleading. On the other hand, in other situations the youth worker might feel pressured to focus exclusively on the helping role because they fear many young people would have nothing to do with them if they thought their disclosures might be reported to police or other authorities.

These dilemmas are real ones for direct practice workers. However, it seems that the more effective workers are able to strike a balance between the social control and welfare functions. There is some research evidence suggesting that an approach which achieves this balance is likely to be of most benefit to involuntary clients. For example, some years ago, I undertook a review of new books on community corrections programs around the world (Trotter 1996b). These books suggest that many programs focus on welfare or punishment rather than a combination of the two. The books point to the importance of a balanced approach if programs are to be successful.

Similarly, in child protection work, getting the balance right between welfare and social control is important. Lawrence Shulman (1991) found that effective child protection workers focused on and emphasised the dual nature of their role in discussions with clients. This was also supported in my child protection study. The clients were inclined to see their workers either as helpers or investigators—as friends or enemies. Yet, when they described their workers as both helpers and investigators, those clients had better outcomes. Similarly, when the child protection workers talked to clients about their dual role as both helper and investigator, those clients also had better outcomes (Trotter 2004).

There will always be occasions in work with involuntary clients when either the welfare or legalistic aspects of the worker's role predominate for a part of, or even for the duration of, work with a particular client. However, even in situations where the focus of the work is on legalistic issues—such as the first child protection visit—it is important for the client to understand that the worker also has a helping role. The early child protection interviews can begin to prepare clients for the problem-solving process which may follow.

Lawrence Shulman, in his book on child protection in Canada, gives an example of the type of comments about the dual role which might be made by a worker on an initial visit: 'I am here because we received a call from someone who felt you might be neglecting your child. I have to investigate such calls to see if there is any truth in them. I also want to see if there is any way we might be helpful to you.' (Shulman 1991:27) The worker might then go on to discuss with the client how they can help, and explain what 'to investigate' actually means.

Similar comments can be made to other involuntary clients. For example, a probation officer might comment: 'My job involves making sure you carry out the conditions of the court order. It is also an equally important part of my work to help you with any problems which might have caused you to be put on probation.'

To sum up: workers with involuntary clients are likely to be more effective if they acknowledge the difficulties inherent in their dual role as social controllers and helpers, and if they help their clients to understand the nature of this dual role. Frequent and regular discussion with clients about this issue, along with the other role-related issues addressed below, is likely to lead to improved outcomes for clients.

# What is negotiable and what is not?

In helping clients to understand the nature of the dual role of the worker, the worker and client will often discuss negotiable and non-negotiable aspects of the intervention. Involuntary clients should be clear about what is required of them, and what the likely consequences are if they do not comply with those requirements. They should be clear about whether these are legal requirements, organisational requirements or worker requirements.

For example, a child protection worker working with a family on a court order may have power to remove a child in certain circumstances. In what circumstances might this happen? Would a further incidence of physical assault automatically result in this occurring? Are there other 'bottom lines' with which the parent must comply to keep the child? Can the parents use other forms of discipline with the child— for example, is any smacking acceptable?

Similar questions can be asked in relation to probation. A probationer is required to report to his probation officer on a regular basis. What happens if the probationer fails to report? What if he misses one, two or three appointments? What if he has a good reason for being unable to attend? When the probationer does report, what is required of him? Is involvement in a problem-solving process with the worker voluntary or involuntary? What if the probationer chooses to attend as required, but only gives basic information and refuses to discuss personal issues? In other words, does the client have a right to refuse treatment? What if the probationer wishes to go on holidays? Can he make up appointments by doing two in one week rather than one each week?

These issues also arise in settings where clients might be considered more voluntary. For example, a school welfare worker or school counsellor might be asked to work with a student displaying behavioural problems in class following the separation of his parents. Does the student have to see the counsellor? What will happen if he fails to do so? What will be the consequences if the student sees the counsellor but refuses to discuss issues with her? Does the student have a right to stop the counsellor talking to the student's parents?

Lloyd Owen and Denbigh Richards (1995) consider negotiable and non-negotiable areas from a slightly different perspective in terms of legally or voluntarily derived mandates for intervention. They point out that it is important for the client to understand whether non-negotiable requirements are based on a legal mandate, an organisational expectation or simply a worker's expectations. For example, a probation officer might have a legal mandate to require a probationer to report regularly; however, she might have an organisational mandate to work with the client on issues which relate to the offending behaviour.

Failure to work on drug-related issues, for example, might not in this instance lead to a return of the matter to court, but it might lead to increased frequency of appointments imposed by the probation service.

Work with involuntary clients involves being clear about negotiable and non-negotiable areas, and about legally and non-legally derived mandates for intervention. In many instances, clients may be concerned about these issues but may not be sufficiently aware or confident to articulate them. In most cases, it is up to the worker to raise them and to help the client to understand them.

# Confidentiality

Confidentiality in work with involuntary clients is perhaps a misleading notion. Who can know and who cannot is a more meaningful way of talking about what happens to information passed from clients to workers.

In work with involuntary clients, information given by the client to the worker is often passed on to other places. It might, for example, be used in court reports; it might be discussed with the worker's supervisor; it might be used in case planning meetings within the worker's organisation; or it might be passed on to other agencies, such as drug or psychiatric treatment agencies.

Some matters which are discussed between workers and their clients might be confidential—in other words, information about the discussion may not be passed on to anyone. For example, a mental health client might discuss with his worker his feelings of depression and worthlessness, and his inability to relate to women. The worker might work through this issue with the client on the understanding that it is confidential—or at least that any discussion about these issues with another professional would not take place without prior discussion with and agreement from the client.

The issue of who can know should be discussed with clients in some detail. An open exploration of these issues is an important part of effective work with involuntary clients.

# File notes

File notes may be a source of concern in work with involuntary clients. Sometimes uncertainty surrounds what access the client has to file notes. In many public welfare agencies, clients and client families accumulate large files. Often they run to two or more volumes. In some instances, they contain many more words than an average book. In practice situations, workers sometimes bring those paper files into the interview rooms with their clients. It would be surprising if clients did not feel some curiosity or even anxiety about the material in these files.

There are instances where it may not be appropriate to allow clients to read their files—for example, if they contain reports written by professionals other than the current worker. The casual comment in a file note that a particular client was adopted or that the client's estranged father was in prison could be devastating to a young person who is unaware of these things. Care must, of course, be exercised in these situations.

As a general rule, however, the sharing of file notes with clients is recommended as consistent with the principles of effective practice. It is argued in Chapter 5 that sharing file notes can be used to assist in the problem-solving process.

Clients are also likely to be interested in who else can read their files. Often, in work with involuntary clients, courts can subpoena files and workers can be cross-examined in relation to the content of files. Senior staff also have access to files, as do other staff members, including clerical staff. In many agencies, files are described as the property of the agency and access is available to most if not all agency staff.

Revelations about all the people who might have access to client files might raise anxiety in some clients. It is certainly not recommended that the worker necessarily detail all the people who might have access to a client file. Nonetheless, an open approach to this issue is part of effective practice.

Discussion with clients in general terms about the limited nature of confidentiality in relation to files and other information should be a routine part of work with involuntary clients. If, for example, excerpts from a file are read to a court, this should not be a surprise to the client. The worker should have discussed such a possibility at some time during the period of contact with the client.

The research discussed in Chapter 2 suggests that open, honest and frequent discussions about issues such as these are important to effective practice. Good practice with involuntary clients involves being sensitive to client concerns and discussing issues about confidentiality on a regular basis.

# Case manager, case planner or problem-solver?

Another issue which should be addressed with clients relates to the worker's role as case manager, case planner and problem-solver. In Chapter 1, direct practice was defined as the provision of direct problem-solving or counselling services to clients in addition to planning, oversight and referral. Case management, on the other hand, was defined more in terms of oversight and referral functions.

The worker should be clear about their particular role as a case planner, case manager or problem-solver. They should also help the client to understand the role of other workers in the helping process. In addition, the worker should explore the client's perceptions of the worker's role and help the client to understand the different aspects of that role.

This involves the worker helping the client to understand the specific tasks for which the worker is responsible. If the worker has a role as a case manager and case planner, with much of the direct problem-solving work being done by other agencies or workers, this should be made clear to the client. The worker should try to help the client understand how help will be provided for different problems, how services will be coordinated and the worker's responsibilities in this, what the client can do if services are unsatisfactory, and what happens if the client does not follow up services as planned.

It should also be clear to the client how they can participate in the case-management, case-planning and problem-solving processes. The client should be helped to understand his role in relation to each step of each of the processes.

# The client's expectations

Clients may have had experience of casework services before. They may have had a number of different workers from different parts of the public welfare system. They may have developed expectations—realistic or unrealistic—about the nature of the role of the worker. Such expectations might have derived from a culture which is different from that familiar to the worker. The notion of a direct practice worker having a helping role might seem foreign to clients with particular cultural backgrounds. An exploration of these expectations will help the worker and the client to clarify the nature of the worker's role.

There may be instances when clients make reference to previous workers. For example, a probationer might say: 'My last worker did not seem too interested in talking about my problems. All she cared about was whether I turned up for appointments.' The worker might use these comments to explore the client's expectations of the probation officer's role.

The worker might comment: 'I also believe it is absolutely essential that you turn up for appointments. However, I am concerned about other things you do. In fact, as I have explained, I hope we can work on some other issues that seem to have led to you being placed on probation. Have you ever had a probation officer who helped you with your problems?'

A probation client may be in contact with other offenders and may have developed perceptions of probation supervision from their comments. The probationer might have heard, for example, that it is possible to get away with missing every second appointment if you ring each time and make an excuse. In order to explore these issues, the probation officer might ask the client what they know about probation, how often they would expect to report, and so on. The probation officer might also ask the client if friends have been on probation and what their experiences were.

If clients have misconceptions about the nature of the worker's role, it is important that these are explored. When I started work in probation, I was surprised by the number of probationers who simply failed to keep appointments and failed to notify any change of address. In due course they would be arrested, and I would visit them in prison. In many cases, they would say they just wanted to get away and did not realise that probation supervision could be transferred. On other occasions, they had missed one appointment and thought that this would automatically result in revocation of their probation. Their misconceptions led to the cancellation of their probation and to their subsequent imprisonment.

Another example from foster care illustrates this point. A thirteen-year-old girl had been placed in numerous children's homes and foster homes. On one occasion, she was abused by her foster parents. She was unable to convince her worker at the time that the placement was unsuitable and she subsequently ran away. In discussions with the new worker about what she expected from the worker, she mentioned her disappointment with the previous worker. The new worker was then able to address these concerns and reassure the young person that it was part of the role of the worker to respond and follow up situations such as these. The worker was able to point out that if such a situation were to be repeated, the client should contact the worker immediately rather than simply running away.

Effective work with involuntary clients involves understanding what the client expects from the intervention and clarifying misconceptions. This sometimes involves exploring the client's earlier experiences.

# Helping the client to understand the nature of the professional relationship

Clients and workers often have differing views about the extent to which the worker and client are friends and the extent to which the worker is an advocate for the client. A client who might comment in relation to his worker: 'You are my friend and I can count on you to be on my side' may be disappointed if the worker is forced to take action with which the client disagrees.

My study in the probation area (Trotter 1993) asked clients to describe the role of their supervisor. They were given a number of options to choose from, including supervisor, friend, advocate, counsellor, adviser, police officer and prison officer. Forty-seven per cent described the probation officer as their friend, after supervisor (61 per cent) and counsellor (51 per cent). I found a very similar response in my child protection study (Trotter 2004). In fact, more than half of the adolescent child protection clients described their workers as their friend. It seems likely that there was a lack of congruence in relation to worker and client views about this issue. Few workers would describe their clients as friends.

In work with adolescents who may have few identity models, with clients experiencing depression or other mental illness, with isolated parents or victims of domestic violence, the potential for clients to look for more in the client–worker relationship than the worker intends is always present.

This confusion about the extent to which the worker is a friend or a professional can create particular problems with long-term and dependent clients. The issue of dependency can present as much difficulty in work with involuntary clients as issues relating to resistance. This relates in part to the fact that work with involuntary clients is often long term. Indeed, there are many instances of children being involved in the child welfare system for the bulk of their childhood and adolescence. Workers involved with families or individuals over long periods, particularly when those families and individuals lead isolated lives, have to deal regularly with the issue of dependence.

Appropriate role clarification involves the worker exploring with the client the issue of friendship and the client's expectations in this area. Before this can occur, workers of course need to be clear in their own minds about the limits of the relationship. Discussion can then take place in relation to these limits. For example, it is generally appropriate to discuss the fact that the worker is employed by an agency for a specific purpose; therefore the worker has a number of clients, and the time they have available is limited. The worker should be clear about the extent to which they are available to talk to or visit the client between scheduled appointments.

Discussions about the nature of the direct practice process and the purpose of the intervention will also help the client to understand the limits of the relationship. The intervention process itself should involve a clear plan with specific strategies and a proposed time of termination. Even in long-term interventions, the work should be broken down into stages. For example, the worker might work towards a set of goals with a drug-addicted mother over a period of three months. After the three months have elapsed, a review of progress can take place and another agreement reached to work toward other goals for the next three months. This is consistent with effective practice as outlined in Chapter 2, and avoids the unstructured supportive type of worker–client relationship which may well foster client dependency.

In work with isolated clients, it is important that the issue of isolation is dealt with directly. It is clearly preferable that a client develop new social networks with the help of the worker rather than the worker fulfilling these needs.

The best protection against inappropriate client dependency (and, for that matter, worker dependency) is the regular and frequent discussion about the role-related issues raised in this chapter and the use of a structured problem-solving approach as outlined in Chapter 5.

# Organisational expectations

It can be difficult for workers to come to terms with their role in their organisation. In some organisations, direct practice workers get clear messages from their organisations about their role. They may have opportunities to provide input to the organisation in relation to role-related issues. For example, staff members might regularly discuss issues with each other and senior staff relating to the welfare and social control aspects of the work. In other organisations, workers may receive confused messages about their role and they may feel powerless to influence the direction of the organisation.

A working environment which helps workers to explore issues relating to their role is likely to produce workers who help clients explore issues relating to the worker's role—leading, in turn, to more effective work. There is support for this view in Lawrence Shulman's (1991) child protection study and my child protection study (Trotter 2004), both of which suggested that when supervisors talked about their role with workers under their supervision, those workers were more inclined to talk abut their role with their clients.

Some of the organisational issues which workers might discuss with their clients include: What relationship does the worker have with the employing organisation? Does the employing organisation place restraints on the way the worker functions—for example, does the worker receive supervision and does the supervision influence decisions the worker makes? Or does the organisation have particular policies— for example, does the organisation have a policy about the right of clients to change workers? Does the organisation require workers to complete a risk assessment profile on clients? Or a more specific example: Does the organisation have a policy about excluding men from group counselling if they make threats of physical violence within the group?

Discussion about the policies of the organisation, how these impact on the workers and how they impact on the clients is all part of the role-clarification process.

# Theoretical approach to the work

Many of the readers of this book, if they were to seek the services of a professional counsellor, would insist on knowing something of that person's background and theoretical approach. They might want to know what qualifications the counsellor had, the particular theoretical approach they worked from, the amount of experience they had in this type of work or whether they had helped previous clients.

Involuntary clients may not be so demanding or articulate; nevertheless, they may have an interest in the particular approach the worker uses. Ivanoff, Blythe and Tripodi (1994), in their book about involuntary clients, comment that 'the client has a right to understand the theoretical premises that guide the practitioner's choice of intervention' (1994:58).

In clarifying their roles, workers should be open about their particular theoretical approaches and provide opportunities for clients to ask questions about them. If, for example, the worker is using a problem-solving approach, it is appropriate to explain this to the client. This might involve a brief comment in a first interview but more detailed explanation in subsequent interviews.

Following training courses I have undertaken with workers dealing with involuntary clients, some workers have displayed in their offices a list of steps relating to the collaborative problem-solving model referred to in Chapter 5. On some occasions they have taken posters displaying the steps to client's homes. They then work through the various steps, explaining to clients the structure they are using for the interviews. This is certainly an approach I favour because it is consistent with the principle of giving clients maximum information about the direct practice process and their part in it.

# Case examples

The following examples of interviews or conversations between workers and involuntary clients illustrate an approach to the clarification of role which is consistent with the principles of effective practice. The conversations are simple, and some readers may feel that 'this is what they would have done anyway', evidenced-based practice or not. It is my belief, however—having observed many interviews conducted by experienced workers—that these skills are harder to apply than they at first appear to be.

The interviews in this chapter, and in subsequent chapters, are in some cases based on actual clients with details changed to protect their anonymity. In other cases, the interviews have been constructed by professional workers through role plays and collaboration with myself.

## A first interview between a child protection worker and a father who has been leaving his children unsupervised

The child protection worker in this example has received a report that the client, Jake, has on many occasions left his two children, aged five and three, at home without supervision, sometimes for several hours. The child protection worker has visited with a colleague to investigate the report. The worker is trying to help the client to understand her role as a child protection worker.

*Worker:* Jake, I'm Janet Smith. Thank you for giving me the opportunity to come in and talk to you a little bit more about why I'm here.

*Jake:* OK.

*Worker:* As I said to you at the front door, I'm part of the child protection team at the Department of Human Services. Have you had anything to do with child protection before? Do you know what we do?

*Jake:* Are they the people who take children away?

*Worker:* That is what a lot of people think—that our job is to come and take children away. However, this happens in a very small number of cases. The vast bulk of our work is with helping families. When we receive a report that children might be at risk, then we come out to see what's happening, and to see if there's anything that the family needs that we can help them with. So there are two roles. Number one is, are the children safe? And number two, what can we help the family with?

*Jake:* I know someone that was involved with child protection, and they didn't receive help. What they received was a lot of investigation and eventually the child was taken away for a week and then brought back again. You wouldn't believe the problems they had. And it seemed to me they'd done nothing. Has someone complained about my children?

*Worker:* Well, someone's raised concerns about your children, and obviously if you know someone who's had a negative experience I guess that could make you anxious to know what we're going to say and do in relation to you.

*Jake:* Yeah.

*Worker:* What we'll be doing is talking with you about what is happening—whether there's anything that is putting your children's safety at risk, and whether there's anything we can help you with. I also need to let you know that we usually work in pairs and we always take notes because there is a very small number of cases in which the matter is taken to the Children's Court and sometimes the information that we gain when we talk with families is used as part of a court report.

*Jake:* So this information is being written down.

*Worker:* Yes, we always record initial interviews.

*Jake:* And it can be used in court?

*Worker:* It can be.

*Jake:* Are you saying that I could have to go to court?

*Worker:* What I'm saying is that in a very small number of cases, perhaps 5 per cent of the total number of calls that we get, a matter might be taken to the Children's Court if we feel a child is immediately, seriously at risk of harm.

*Jake:* Well, my children are fine.

*Worker:* OK, so if your children are not immediately, seriously at risk of harm, then you wouldn't need to be concerned. Then our role is to talk to you about what has been said, and to explore with you what difficulties you might have and how we might be able to help you overcome them. Hopefully this helps you as a parent and helps your children as well.

*Jake:* This wasn't what happened to this friend of mine; no one came to help her.

*Worker:* So the experience with your friend was that there was a lot of investigation and no help?

*Jake:* Yes, the child was taken away for a week, and brought back again, and then after about two months she didn't even hear or see anyone from child protection.

*Worker:* Sorry. I can't comment on what happened in that case because I don't know the family, I don't know the situation. All I can do is deal with you in this situation and tell you what my role is, and what we'll be doing with your family. And we prefer as much as possible to work together with families.

*Jake:* So can you help with things like babysitters and that sort of thing?

*Worker:* We can do a lot to help with getting referrals to services to get that sort of thing. There's a broad range of things that we can do. Part of it is ensuring the children's safety and part of it is to help you as a parent to look after your children.

*Jake:* Well, who's making this complaint?

*Worker:* I'm not allowed to tell you who has made the complaint, that's protected information, but I can tell you what the information was that we were given in the report.

*Jake:* The neighbour next door. She would have done it. She doesn't like me.

*Worker:* I can't comment on who has or who hasn't made the complaint.

*Jake:* Well, she's mad, do you know that?

*Worker:* OK, you may feel that your neighbour did it. I can't say who has made the report; all I can say is what the concerns are, and then we can decide whether the concerns are real or not, and if there is some problem what we can do—how we can work together to resolve it.

*Jake:* How are you going to know if anything's happened? What's supposed to have happened anyway?

*Worker:* Well, the first thing we do is talk to you, we talk to your children, and we also would like to talk to some other professionals who might be involved or somebody else who might help us know what is happening with your children. Now, we often talk with schools. They can tell us a lot about how things are with a family.

*Jake:* So you're going to be talking to the school about all this, are you?

*Worker:* If we can get your permission to talk to the school, that would be very helpful to us.

*Jake:* You won't talk to the school without my permission?

*Worker:* What we'll be doing first is asking for your permission to talk with the school. If it ever happens that a parent refuses permission to talk and we feel that we still need to, then I will tell you if we're going to do that.

*Jake:* So you can talk to the school anyway.

*Worker:* Not necessarily, it depends on the situation. Each situation is decided on its merits.

*Jake:* Can you tell me what the complaint is?

*Worker:* Yes, the concern is that you've been leaving your children, who I understand to be three and five—is that right? That you've been leaving them on their own at home for considerable periods of time—up to a couple of hours.

*Jake:* Well, that's not true.

*Worker:* So, does it ever happen? That they're left alone at home?

*Jake:* They are left at home for very short periods, when I need to do the shopping. I've got to feed them. I've had these children for the last two years, since the baby was still in nappies and their mother left two years ago. I've been doing all the work for them. I'm the one that's been changing the nappies, doing the shopping, doing the work.

*Worker:* And it's hard work.

*Jake:* Have you got children?

*Worker:* No, I haven't. I work with children and families a lot, though, and what I do know is that being a single parent, and looking after children on your own, is a very tough job. Being a parent is a tough job, but doing it on your own, when you haven't got backup, is even harder.

In this interview, the worker is trying to help the client understand her welfare/investigatory role. By initially talking to the client about previous experiences, rather than launching into a description of her role, the worker is able to identify misapprehensions which the client might have about the role of the child protection worker and to deal with the client's fear that the children might be removed.

## *A second interview between a probation officer and an eighteen-year-old male client*

In this case study, the probation officer and client are exploring issues relating to appointments. The probation officer is trying to ensure that the probationer, Tom, understands what reporting as required means.

*Probation officer (PO):* I would like to do a quick review of the probation order before we do anything else.

*Tom:* OK.

*PO:* Do you understand what is meant by being required to report to the probation officer as and when required?

*Tom:* Yes. It means I have to come here when you say so.

*PO:* That's right, Tom. However, if you are unable to keep an appointment and you ring me up and give me an explanation then it might be OK to change the time of the appointment.

*Tom:* So if I want to go to the night football I could ring you?

*PO:* No. It would be most unusual for anyone to change an appointment because of a football match. You could ring and ask, however. That is the sort of thing that might be OK once you have established a regular pattern of reporting— perhaps after three or four months.

*Tom:* When can I miss appointments, then?

*PO:* When it is something that might help you keep out of trouble or some sort of emergency—if you were asked to work overtime or if a family member was very ill. But you would still need to ring and let me know that you couldn't come.

*Tom:* What happens if I don't ring?

*PO:* You have been on probation before. What was your experience then?

*Tom:* The PO said I could not miss appointments but he did nothing about it when I did.

*PO:* Well I am different from that. If you miss an appointment without speaking to me first and you cannot provide a good explanation—for example, that you were sick and you have a doctor's certificate—then I give you a formal warning and that goes in the file. If you receive three formal warnings in the next six months, I have to refer to my senior probation officer, who will make a decision about whether to return the matter to court. Do you think you will have any problem keeping appointments?

*Tom:* I might, because I come here on a bus and sometimes the buses don't come.

*PO:* What could you do if that happened?

*Tom:* I guess I could ring you and make another time.

*PO:* That would be good. Could you bring in the bus timetable next time and I will try to schedule appointments so they fit in with the bus schedule?

*Tom:* OK.

*PO:* Are you likely to have any other problems keeping these appointments?
*Tom:* No, I don't think so.

This is a short excerpt, and it seems mundane. To suggest that the worker is displaying role-clarification skills in this interview might seem surprising. However, the research cited in this chapter and in Chapter 2 suggests that a willingness to explore these very practical issues with clients is related to positive outcomes.

Probationers may develop misapprehensions about reporting requirements through previous experience, contact with other offenders or lack of information, and those misapprehensions can lead to failure to comply with the probation order. If the client understands what reporting as required means, and if he is given an opportunity to examine issues which might make it difficult for him to fulfil the requirements, he is likely to be in a better position to comply with the order and less likely to develop resentment which might arise from any misunderstanding.

The skill of role clarification for the most part is not complex. It is apparent, however, that when workers with involuntary clients devote time to it their clients do better.

# Summary

Direct practice with involuntary clients involves ongoing and frequent exploration with the client about the specific role of the worker and the part the client plays in the process. This chapter has highlighted a number of specific issues relating to role which should be addressed routinely in work with involuntary clients. These include: the dual (social control/welfare) role of the worker; what is negotiable and not negotiable, and how the worker's authority might be used; the client's expectations of the worker; confidentiality and who has a right to information; the nature of the professional relationship and what this means in terms of how the worker and client interact; the role of the worker as case manager, case planner or problem-solver/counsellor; the client's expectations of the casework process; the expectations the worker's employing organisation places on the worker and the client; and the theoretical approach the worker takes to the work.

Some of these issues are more relevant in some situations than others. It may not be appropriate, for example, to discuss all these issues in short-term contacts with involuntary clients. It does appear, however, that more effective workers devote time and energy to the clarification of role.

# 4 PROMOTING PRO-SOCIAL OUTCOMES

The practice model presented in this book proposes that workers make use of the following skills in their work with involuntary clients: they work on ensuring that the client understands the role of the worker, particularly the dual social control and welfare role; they make use of the skills of pro-social modelling and reinforcement in order to encourage and promote client pro-social values and behaviours; they attempt to work with clients using a collaborative problem-solving approach which focuses on client definitions of problems and client goals; and they make use of relationship skills such as self-disclosure, empathy, optimism and humour. It is proposed that workers use these skills in an explicit and open manner.

In Chapter 2, I suggested that the term 'pro-social practice' is often used to describe the intervention model as a whole, including each of these skills. Pro-social modelling and reinforcement, or the pro-social approach, constitute one aspect of pro-social practice. Pro-social modelling and reinforcement, like the other approaches described in this book, is based on the research about effective practice which shows it to be an effective method of working with involuntary clients (Andrews et al. 1979; Andrews and Bonta 2003; Trotter 1996a, 2004). In fact, in my study in corrections, it was clearly the most influential worker skill. Where workers made frequent use of the pro-social approach, their clients were imprisoned at about half the rate of clients of workers who made infrequent use of the approach, even after four years. Similar positive outcomes were seen in my child protection study (Trotter 2004).

The approach is based on learning theory. It centres on the belief that people are influenced by behaviour which is modelled by others and by positive and negative reinforcement of their own behaviour. A lot has been written, particularly in psychology, about learning theory and its application to counselling situations (e.g. Andrews and Bonta 2003; Watt, Howells and Delfabbro 2004; Burton and Meezan 2004).

Some basic behavioural principles include: behaviour is more likely to be maintained or developed if it is rewarded; the promise of a reward does not work as well as simply providing the actual reward following an occurrence of the particular behaviour; rewards are more effective if they are no greater than they need to be; rewards work best if they are perceived as fair in the circumstances; intrinsic rewards (those which exist in a client's natural environment) work best and foster continuation of the rewarded behaviour; and variable rewards which provide reinforcement on an irregular basis are likely to be more effective than continuous or fixed-ratio rewards.

While these principles are relevant to pro-social modelling and reinforcement, use of this approach does not require workers to have a detailed understanding of learning theory. It simply involves a recognition that clients are likely to respond to modelling, rewards and punishments, and that workers should be aware of the nature of the models, rewards and punishments they offer.

Pro-social modelling and reinforcement, as used in my studies (Trotter 1996a, 2004) and the study by Don Andrews and his colleagues (1979), asked workers to:

- identify positive or pro-social comments or behaviours as they occurred in their interaction with clients;
- reward those comments and behaviours wherever possible, most often by the use of praise;
- model pro-social expressions and actions; and
- challenge anti-social or pro-criminal comments or behaviours.

The particular advantages and disadvantages of this approach are discussed later in this chapter. Outlined below is some more detail about the practical implementation of the approach, illustrated by examples from child protection.

# Identifying pro-social comments and actions

During the course of interviews, workers should try to identify their client's pro-social comments and behaviours. This, of course, involves the worker thinking about the things that they would like their clients to be saying and doing.

In most cases, the nature of pro-social comments is fairly clear. Some examples include: comments by an abusive parent which recognise the harm that abuse of children can cause, or the harm that has been done by the specific behaviours of the parent; statements that recognise children have feelings and developmental needs—for example, a comment by an abusive parent that her child was very upset after she was smacked; statements recognising the physical needs of children—for example, comments that babies' nappies should be changed regularly; comments which recognise that the client would like to develop improved parenting skills; comments suggesting ways that parenting skills could be improved; statements recognising that the worker is concerned about the child's welfare; or comments supporting a case plan developed in relation to the particular family. In some instances, pro-social comments might also include interest in social activities or expressing interest in attending educational courses (e.g. for an isolated person).

Pro-social behaviours are similar—for example, parents changing nappies regularly; using non-physical means to discipline children; undertaking a parenting skills course; arranging access with an estranged parent; talking to a child about feelings; showing interest in a child's schooling; attending an educational course; attending a case-planning meeting; or simply attending a meeting with the worker.

There are other instances when what is pro-social and what is not pro-social is more difficult to determine. Take, for example, a mother who has neglected her children and has now developed a new re-lationship with a man. She comments to the worker that her new partner is helping her to discipline her children and has smacked one of them. It may be a positive thing for the mother to have developed the relationship and good that her partner is interested in her child. However, the worker may not wish to encourage the use of physical punishment, particularly by a new partner.

Another example relates to a thirteen-year-old girl who has been admitted to care after having run away from home on numerous occasions. She approaches her worker saying that she wants to do something about birth control because she is worried that she could become pregnant. Again, being concerned about not getting pregnant may be pro-social but having sexual relations at such a young age may not be.

Or again, a young person comments to his worker that he is staying away from heroin but still uses marijuana. Not using heroin may be pro-social but views might vary about the extent to which use of marijuana is pro-social.

Workers themselves hold a wide variety of views in relation to various ethical issues. We have, no doubt, all worked or interacted with people with whom we strongly disagree on a range of moral and value-based issues.

It could be that the use of pro-social modelling and reinforcement might lead to the imposition of particular values on clients by some workers. This issue is discussed later in the chapter. At this stage, however, I will consider the other steps in pro-social modelling and reinforcement.

# Providing rewards

The next step is to provide rewards or reinforcement for pro-social actions and comments. The most powerful reward or reinforcer available to the worker is praise. The pro-social approach involves the frequent use of praise for pro-social actions and comments. If, for example, a client attends a case-planning meeting, the social worker should make it clear that this is a good thing. Praise should be used liberally, but purposefully. It should be directed towards the pro-social comments and actions of the client, rather than simply being offered indiscriminately.

Attending for appointments, for example, is a pro-social action which should be rewarded. The idea would be to say to the client: 'It is good that you were able to get here on time today and that you have been able to get to our last couple of appointments; it is clear that you are taking the whole thing seriously', rather than simply saying: 'It is good to see you today.' The idea is to identify any pro-social acts or comments and praise them liberally—remembering, of course, that the praise is only likely to be effective if it appears genuine to the client.

Again using the child protection example, there are a number of rewards which might be used to encourage pro-social comments and actions. For example: visiting a client at home rather than expecting the client to visit the office (or vice versa, depending on the view of the client); referring the client to other agencies; reducing the frequency of contact or in some instances spending more time with clients; visiting at times the client chooses; organising financial assistance; or organising practical assistance for a client, such as home maintenance, furniture or transport.

A good illustration of the way rewards can be used to reinforce behaviour relates to the place in which an interview is held. In deciding to conduct an interview in McDonald's, for example, rather than in the worker's office, the worker may be providing a reward to the client (particularly if the client also gets a free lunch). If the client is left to think that this is simply routine, then an opportunity is lost. Rather, using the pro-social approach, the worker would make it clear that the interview is being conducted away from the office because the client prefers this. The worker would point out that she is happy to put herself out in this way because the client has, for example, kept appointments regularly, followed up a referral to a parenting group and has openly discussed problems with the worker. The client in this instance gets a sense that doing the things that the worker wants will help to get what she (the client) wants.

Taking the converse situation of a client who is not reporting regularly and is being generally uncooperative, if the worker in this instance decides to see the client in McDonald's in the hope that the client will be more cooperative, and this is in some way communicated to the client, then the client may get a sense that her uncooperative behaviour has led to a reward. The uncooperative behaviour is thereby reinforced and is more likely to continue.

A qualitative study undertaken in corrections found that workers often inadvertently reinforced the very things they were trying to prevent (Burns 1994). For example, one worker made the following comment: 'We are getting nowhere with these interviews and I think we should see each other less often in the future.' This comment represents a clear reward for uncooperative (not pro-social) behaviour.

It is sometimes argued in seminars I have conducted that these things are rights rather than rewards, and should not be dispensed as rewards. However, in reality workers make discretionary decisions about these issues on a day-to-day basis. If clients feel that the worker is just as likely to reward them if they make anti-social or pro-criminal comments, then their anti-social behaviour is more likely to continue. On the other hand, if it is clear to the client that positive behaviours and attitudes can lead to the things they want, then they are more likely to make use of them.

The role of the worker is to ensure that the reward system works in this way. In many cases, it is simply a matter of the worker being explicit about the reasons for a particular action being taken. If the frequency of contact is reduced, for example, then it is generally because of progress of some sort on the part of the client. It is simply a matter of making this explicit.

Another method by which clients can be rewarded is through the use of file notes or letters. Workers might make notes about the positive things that clients have done and share these with the client. It might be highlighted in file notes, for example, that the client has kept appointments regularly, attended for case-planning meetings and followed up referrals for drug rehabilitation. Consequently, the frequency of contact with the worker is to be reduced. Similarly, progress reports, final reports or letters to clients can be used to highlight the progress and pro-social actions of clients.

Through the reinforcement process, it seems that clients learn the behaviours and attitudes which the worker is trying to promote. It is apparent from my research in corrections and child protection (Trotter 1996a, 2004) that the behaviours are learned quickly (within a few months), and sustained over the long term. As I mentioned earlier, reduced reoffending rates following the use of this approach in probation supervision continued to be seen in my study even after four years, despite the fact that supervision for the most part ceased within one year (Trotter 1996a).

# Modelling pro-social behaviours

The third aspect of pro-social modelling and reinforcement relates to modelling pro-social behaviours. Modelling pro-social behaviours involves the worker modelling the behaviour that they wish to foster in the client. Again using child protection to illustrate the principle, the worker should be available when they are supposed to be, or should ring to change appointments; they should treat the family with the same respect with which they hope the family members will treat their children; they should speak positively about their own children; they should express views about the importance of children receiving good care; and they should show empathy for the children's situation and similarly show empathy for the parents' situation (without condoning anti-social behaviours in any way).

The worker should also be reliable, responding promptly to phone calls from clients, keeping appointments with clients, being punctual and doing the things they have said they would do. As I mentioned in Chapter 2, workers in my child protection study who were reliable in this way had clients with good outcomes—the clients were satisfied with the child protection experience, the workers reported that their clients progressed well and cases were closed early (Trotter 2004).

Some degree of self-disclosure may be appropriate in presenting as a pro-social model. For example, a worker might comment on how difficult she found it when her children were young although she always managed to avoid using physical punishment. In this type of modelling, it is important not to appear to be smug or have all the answers. In fact, a useful distinction can be made between 'coping' modelling as opposed to modelling which suggests that the worker has all the answers (Masters et al. 1987; Andrews and Bonta 2003). Coping modelling, which reveals the worker's vulnerability and acknowledges the difficulty which the worker has experienced, seems to work better.

The appropriateness of self-disclosure is discussed in Chapters 2 and 6. It is very difficult to be prescriptive about it; nevertheless, it does appear that self-disclosure is one method of modelling and encouraging particular behaviours. For example, Shulman (1991), in his child protection study, refers to the value of using some self-disclosure to encourage clients to open up about issues. Similarly, in our child protection study (Trotter 2004), the client outcomes were more positive if clients felt that their worker used some self-disclosure.

# Challenging undesirable behaviours

The fourth aspect of pro-social modelling and reinforcement relates to challenging pro-criminal, anti-social or undesirable behaviours or comments—for example, comments by clients which attempt to rationalise their anti-social or illegal behaviour. Examples from child protection include: 'I was only disciplining her'; 'I only hit him because he kept crying'; 'A good whack did not do me any harm when I was a child and shouldn't harm anyone today'; or 'I would change the nappies more often if I had a washing machine that worked'.

The child protection worker should identify comments such as these as rationalisations for behaviours which have led the person to become a client of protective services, and then provide some level of negative reinforcement for them. This might include pointing out that the worker does not agree with the comments or simply expressing the view that they are, in fact, rationalisations for unacceptable behaviour.

Care should be taken not to positively reinforce anti-social comments through the inadvertent use of body language, as occurred in many cases in a study of the use of pro-social modelling and re-inforcement in probation by Patrick Burns (1994). Burns found that probation officers often inadvertently reinforced anti-social and pro-criminal comments through the use of body language (e.g. smiling).

Workers should be careful not to respond to rationalisations or anti-social comments with exclusively empathic comments. While rationalisations will inevitably contain some truth (coping with dirty nappies without a washing machine is very difficult, as is coping with crying babies in general), it is important that they are not accepted by the worker as excuses for the behaviour. It must be clear to the client that, while the worker might understand, they don't approve of the excuses for anti-social behaviour.

While it is important that the client understands that the worker does not approve of rationalisations or anti-social comments or actions, it is also important that disapproval and confrontation does not overwhelm the direct practice intervention. This aspect of pro-social practice needs to be used with some caution. It has been suggested in the corrections area—albeit rather arbitrarily—that workers should try to provide at least four positive comments for every negative one (Keissling 1982).

The model as it was implemented in my research (Trotter 1993, 1996a, 2004) focused strongly on positives rather than negatives. The Australian qualitative study by Burns (1994) referred to above also found that more successful probation officers focused almost exclusively on positives, in contrast to less successful officers who were more inclined to focus on negatives.

The need for caution in relation to use of negative reinforcement and confrontation is supported by Shulman, who states in relation to confrontation that:

> analysis of the data on the skills of confrontation thought to be crucial to effective social work practice did not yield the expected supporting results. When it occurs seems to be important. Confrontation which comes too early in the relationship or which is not balanced by a large amount of positive comment may well have a negative impact. (Shulman 1991:11)

This view was supported in our child protection study, which found that the confrontation which worked best involved workers exploring why clients felt the way they did and suggested alternative ways of acting or looking at the situation. Ignoring pro-criminal and anti-social behaviour, or criticising the client, were both related to poor client outcomes (Trotter 2004).

To sum up, it is important in work with involuntary clients that pro-social comments and behaviour are rewarded. It is also important that clients understand that the worker does not approve of anti-social behaviour or rationalisations for it. However, it should also be remembered that people are more likely to learn from positive reinforcement, so workers should focus on the positives.

## Case example

It is interesting to consider the example which was raised in the introduction about clients who come to the office at a different time from their scheduled appointment. On the one hand, workers can argue that they should be sent away because the client should learn responsibility. On the other hand, workers can argue that the client should be seen because it is respectful. What approach should someone take who was using the principles of pro-social modelling and reinforcement?

Let's assume that you, as the worker, wish to encourage the client for coming to see you. However, you do not wish to encourage turning up at unexpected times because it is inconvenient for you. You wish, of course, to model behaviour which is consistent with the behaviour you are seeking from your client. Therefore you talk to the client as promptly as possible. You explain to the client that you are pleased to see him and that you appreciate the fact that he has made the effort to come and see you. You attempt to reward his pro-social action in coming to the office and you model respectful behaviour in talking to the client as soon as possible. You then explain to the client that this is an inconvenient time, and you make another appointment. It is likely that the client will remember the correct appointment next time.

If, on the other hand, you interview the client at the unscheduled time, this will reward his behaviour in turning up unexpectedly and the behaviour is likely to occur again.

In other situations, it might be appropriate to focus on the client's pro-social behaviour in coming to see the worker. Some intellectually disabled, psychiatrically ill or drug-using clients might have difficulty with appointment times. The visit might represent a breakthrough in work with a resistant client. In such an instance, it may be appropriate to see the client and praise the client for attending. This is likely to encourage the client to attend again, even if it is not at the scheduled time.

The worker must think through this issue and decide what behaviour they wish to encourage. In the first example, the worker defines the pro-social behaviour as attending at the scheduled time. In the second example, it is defined as simply attending.

# Advantages of the pro-social approach

The greatest strength of pro-social modelling and reinforcement is that the research evidence suggests it works. It relates to client outcomes with a range of involuntary clients. The evidence from my studies (Trotter 1993, 2004) found that the use of the approach significantly correlated with hard data measures such as reoffending and early case closure in addition to a number of client satisfaction measures. The success of this approach can also be explained theoretically by reference to learning theory.

The pro-social approach works, it seems, because it puts into practice the idea that people learn best by encouragement rather than discouragement. It also provides a method for discouraging and challenging anti-social comments and behaviours within a positive framework.

The approach also helps workers to take control of a reinforcement process which occurs anyway. Whether they are aware of it or not, workers with involuntary clients do make judgments about the things they wish to encourage in their clients, and they do in turn influence their clients' behaviour (Andrews et al. 1979; Burns 1994; Trotter 1990, 1996a, 2004). By understanding the process and using this approach, workers are able to exert control over the nature of this influence.

# Criticisms of the pro-social approach

The relevance of learning theory and of pro-social modelling and re-inforcement in work with involuntary clients is increasingly being recognised in the literature (e.g. Hepworth, Rooney and Larson 2002; Wing Hong and Nellis 2003; Andrews and Bonta 2003). Nevertheless, there are a number of criticisms which may be levelled at the approach. Outlined below are responses to some of these criticisms, and to some of the questions which are often raised in my pro-social modelling workshops.

## What if clients make pro-social comments but their behaviour is inconsistent with their comments?

The aim of the pro-social approach is to reward pro-social behaviour and comments—that is, comments and behaviour which are honest and genuine. A dishonest or frivolous array of comments by an involuntary client about how he has changed should not be defined as pro-social and should not be rewarded, particularly if those comments are not consistent with the client's behaviour.

That said, it can sometimes be difficult to determine whether someone is genuine or not. The worker clearly needs to avoid being 'conned', and should avoid reinforcing behaviour which attempts to do this. Nevertheless, if in doubt, it seems that the most appropriate approach is to accept the client's word—at least until the worker has firm information that what the client is saying is incorrect.

## Don't workers do this anyway?

One of the most frequent comments made in my workshops when this material is presented is 'I do it anyway'. Some workers feel that pro-social modelling and reinforcement merely describe a process which they use unconsciously. However, there is evidence that those who work with involuntary clients do not routinely use these skills. The Canadian corrections study (Andrews et al. 1979) and the Australian studies (Burns 1994; Trotter 1990, 1993, 1996a, 2004) found that workers used pro-social modelling and reinforcement very erratically. Some workers used these techniques and some did not.

My corrections study (Trotter 1993) also saw a clear change in the behaviour of probation officers after they completed training in the use of the approach. As mentioned earlier, Burns' qualitative study undertaken in corrections in Victoria, Australia, found that many probation officers inadvertently reinforced the very behaviour they were hoping to change, often through the use of smiling and body language as much as direct comment or actions (Burns 1994).

There seems little doubt that, while pro-social skills might come naturally to some workers, they do not come naturally to everyone. However, they can be increased through training and by an awareness of them.

One of the strongest arguments in favour of the use of pro-social skills relates to this notion that it occurs anyway. It seems that, whether they are conscious of it or not, to some degree workers reinforce different behaviours in their clients. It is preferable that they are explicit about this process, both with themselves and their clients, and that they take some control over it.

## Is this approach superficial?

It might be argued that the approach is superficial and symptom-focused, and therefore unlikely to address the complex long-term problems of involuntary clients. How could such an approach address issues relating to poverty, unemployment, drug use, depression, and so on? It is certainly true that pro-social modelling and reinforcement will not address all the problems of involuntary clients. They do, however, relate to client outcomes, and can be used along with a range of other skills that might address underlying problems. Clients are influenced by the positive and negative reactions of workers. An understanding of the process, and constructive use of the skills involved, can facilitate movement toward both worker and client goals. This process might seem superficial, but the evidence suggests it is influential.

## Is this approach manipulative?

Pro-social modelling and reinforcement could be viewed as manipulative in that it attempts to change the behaviour of clients in directions set by the worker rather than the client. On the other hand, workers inevitably manipulate clients by encouraging and discouraging certain behaviours. It is far better that this manipulation be explicit than implicit, and that the client and the social worker understand the process.

To ensure that the process is fair, it is particularly important that the worker is open about it. The worker should explain to the client what it involves. The worker should be clear about the goals they are pursuing, and how these might differ from the client's goals. The worker should explain how the reinforcement process will be used to facilitate the achievement of both worker and client goals. As pointed out earlier, effective work with involuntary clients involves an honest and open approach from the worker in relation to issues of authority and role. Where this is present, I believe pro-social practice is less manipulative than traditional approaches with involuntary clients where manipulation may be hidden.

## Doesn't effective practice involve a focus on client goals?

In Chapter 2, I pointed to a number of research studies which suggest that agreement on goals between client and worker is important to effective practice with both voluntary and involuntary clients. Yet the notion of pro-social practice suggests that change can be achieved when workers and clients have different goals.

Wherever possible, workers should work with client goals. In fact, the overriding aim of direct practice—whether or not it involves pro-social modelling and reinforcement, whether clients are involuntary or not—is to reach agreement on goals and, if possible, work with client goals. In many instances in work with involuntary clients, agreement can be reached about goals. However, workers are often confronted with a situation where the client has been referred for behaviours or problems which are either denied or minimised by the client. In fact, in my experience many workers would say this situation is all too common.

In these instances, the worker has certain options: one is to work with the client on goals which the client chooses; another is to be up front about the goals of the worker and the organisation, and to make it explicit that any progress towards these goals will be rewarded and reinforced; or it is possible to use a combination of the two. This third option is consistent with the practice model presented in this book.

In this case, the worker might work with the goals as defined by the client, where these goals are not in conflict with worker goals. At the same time, the worker would simultaneously reinforce progress towards worker and agency goals, such as stopping child abuse, or offending, or domestic violence. The pro-social approach may be used in this way simultaneously with the problem-solving process (see Chapter 5).

Somehow, in work with involuntary clients, workers have to deal with the issue of the different goals held by many of their clients and themselves. Pro-social modelling and reinforcement provide a method for doing this.

## Is this approach judgmental?

The helping professions have often emphasised the need for workers to be non-judgmental (e.g. Heffernan, Shuttlesworth and Ambrosino 1997). Yet the pro-social approach is based on value judgments. The term 'pro-social' has connotations of social control, of there being a right way of doing things, or of what is socially acceptable being best.

Workers with involuntary clients are employed by the state to work with people who have been judged to have transgressed social mores. On a day-to-day basis, they make judgments about unacceptable standards of parenting or acceptable levels of drug use or violence. Direct practice workers make these judgments, they communicate them to clients, and they in turn influence the behaviour of these clients. It should be noted that the corrections studies referred to earlier (Andrews et al. 1979; Trotter 1990, 1993) suggest that workers reinforce different expressions and behaviours, regardless of whether they have any awareness of doing so.

Nevertheless, it is important that pro-social behaviour be defined in explicit and limited terms. It should not be interpreted as meaning having values consistent with the worker. In child protection, for example, it should be defined specifically in terms of behaviours, expressions and attitudes which are consistent with the aim of providing a safe environment for children. As discussed earlier, the Canadian study in corrections (Andrews et al. 1979), unlike the Australian studies (Trotter 1990, 1993), found that supervisors who practised pro-social modelling and reinforcement were only effective if they also practised reflective listening and had high levels of empathy.

It does seem that if pro-social modelling and reinforcement is used in any way as an excuse for moralising on the part of the worker, it will not work. Perhaps one of the strongest arguments for focusing on positives is that it is likely to avoid the possibility that pro-social modelling and reinforcement will come across as moralistic and disapproving.

Working with involuntary clients involves working in a value-laden environment. It is necessary to recognise that this is so, and to encourage debate about how ethical and value-based issues should be dealt with. One of the aims of pro-social modelling and reinforcement is to provide a framework within which these value-based issues can be addressed.

## Is pro-social modelling and reinforcement consistent with feminist and critical theories?

Direct practice with involuntary clients is sometimes criticised because it is seen as supporting the status quo. Many books and articles have been written favouring an approach to direct practice which seeks to change social stereotypes and disadvantage in addition to helping individuals deal with problems (e.g. Dominelli 2002; Mullaly 2002).

It is argued in Chapter 5 that some of these issues can be addressed through the problem-solving process. It was also argued in Chapter 2 that the practice model presented in this book can facilitate a feminist or critical approach to casework. Pro-social modelling and reinforcement, in particular, provides a framework within which feminist or critical principles can be made explicit and promoted. For example, a probation officer might be working with an offender who is on probation for a domestic violence offence and who has a negative attitude towards women. The probation officer, consistent with pro-social practice, would express a goal of changing the client's sexist attitudes. This would be seen as consistent with the overall goal of reduced offending. The probation officer would challenge any sexist comments or rationalisations for sexist behaviour, model non-sexist behaviour and reinforce and reward non-sexist comments made by the client.

Similarly, using pro-social skills a feminist worker working with a female client who lives within a patriarchal family setting would reinforce any comments that the client made which reflected an awareness of her disadvantage as a woman and challenge comments which reflected an acceptance of patriarchal values. The worker would encourage and reward the identification of goals which helped the client to develop independence.

## Is pro-social modelling and reinforcement appropriate across cultures?

Definitions of what is and what is not pro-social are inevitably entrenched in social and cultural mores. For example, female circumcision/genital mutilation may be legal in one culture, yet illegal and viewed as immoral in another. In one country it might be common practice to inflict severe physical punishments on criminal offenders, whereas in another country such practices would be illegal. A family might have a cultural tradition which does not allow young women to go out in the evenings unchaperoned, but the young female client of that family might feel strongly that this is inappropriate. While a worker might define these restrictions on the young person as not pro-social, the parents might argue that the restrictions are pro-social within their culture.

Workers and clients are influenced by their racial, social, religious and economic milieu. Both workers and clients often have strong beliefs about which behaviours might be viewed as pro-social. So who is to decide in these instances what is pro-social and what isn't?

In using pro-social skills, certain principles should apply to guard against the approach becoming a disguise for workers to be moralising and self-righteous. The approach should not provide a method of imposing workers' values on clients.

First, workers should focus on positives. This has already been emphasised and is vital to the effective use of this approach.

Second, confrontation and challenging client behaviour and comments should be limited to issues which relate to the presenting problem (or the mandate for the worker's involvement with the client). For the most part, in the involuntary context, this relates to illegal behaviour—for example, offending, domestic violence, truancy or child abuse. Other 'desirable' behaviours which the worker may wish to encourage, such as seeking employment, developing a relationship, returning to study, developing a more equitable interaction with a partner or visiting estranged children, should be encouraged if the worker believes they are pro-social. The client's failure to do these things should not, however, result in confrontation by the worker.

Third, the direct practice worker should attempt to understand the views and actions of clients in terms of their cultural context. In forming views about what is pro-social in any given situation, the worker should take the client's cultural background into account. This involves talking to the client about cultural differences.

Fourth, workers should examine their own beliefs regarding what is pro-social and what is not, and be explicit about these views with themselves and their clients. Clients should have the option to choose another worker when there are differences in values which make working together too difficult.

## Case example: A perpetrator of domestic violence who has been placed on probation

Con was placed on probation following an assault on his wife which resulted in her hospitalisation and their subsequent separation. This is a transcript of the third interview between the probation officer and Con, who has now returned to live with his wife.

*PO:* It is good to see you. I appreciate your coming on time. It does make things easier for me. Did you come on public transport?

*Con:* Yes. I lost my licence a few months ago.

*PO:* Well, I am pleased to hear that you are not driving. Did you come by train?

*Con:* Train and bus.

*PO:* How long did that take?

*Con:* More than an hour. The bus was late.

*PO:* As I said, I appreciate you making it on time. It has obviously taken some effort. You were saying in the last interview you were thinking of going back home?

*Con:* I am back home now.

*PO:* When did you go home?

*Con:* Last week.

*PO:* How does your wife feel about it?

*Con:* She asked me to come back. She seems all right as long as I keep attending the [domestic violence] groups.

*PO:* I have spoken to the group convener. He said you have been attending but you did miss the first meeting. You have been to two out of three. You seem to be taking this whole thing seriously—attending the groups and coming to these appointments. It is a pity you missed the first one. You must attend eight of the ten sessions or you will have to do the program again.

*Con:* I didn't know that.

*PO:* I mentioned it last week. Is it a problem?

*Con:* No. I have to go because of her anyway.

*PO:* So you're motivated to attend the groups because of your wife's feelings about it?

*Con:* She'll probably ring the cops again if I don't go.

*PO:* The main thing is that you are planning to continue to attend the groups. That is good. Can we talk a bit about the groups? How are you finding them?

*Con:* They're OK. We mostly seem to talk about our feelings or have little lectures about violence.

*PO:* So are you finding them useful?

*Con:* They are OK. Anyway, I know what will happen if I hit her again. Not that I ever did anything more than give her a bit of a slap. But she says if I ever hit her again that will be the end.

*PO:* I understand from reading the police report that you injured your wife quite badly. It certainly was not a bit of a slap. However, I am pleased to hear you say that you won't hit your wife again. Does she mean a lot to you?

*Con:* She does and I didn't want to hit her but she makes me so angry. She says things just to make me mad.

*PO:* You know and I know that that is no excuse for hitting her. Are you saying that you've decided to change your behaviour towards your wife?

*Con:* Well, I know now that I just cannot do it again.

*PO:* I am pleased to hear you say that. I think you're doing pretty well on probation. You have kept most of the appointments and you seem to be determined not to repeat this offence. Seeing you have been doing well, I would be quite happy to come to your house for the next appointment. This will give me a chance to talk to your wife again. In the meantime, I'll ring her about how things are going and about the assistance she is receiving. Now, let's talk more about the situation at home.

In this interview, the worker is trying to praise each pro-social comment or action by Con. She praises his punctual attendance, his not driving while his licence is suspended, the effort he has made to get to the interview, the attendance at two of the domestic violence groups and his motivation to continue attending because of his wife's wishes, his apparent changed behaviour with his wife, and his assertion that he will not hit her again. The probation officer offers to visit the client at home for the next visit, which will save the client a lot of time and effort. She links this to his good response to probation.

She also makes it clear that she does not approve of a number of Con's comments and actions. These include the missed domestic violence group and the minimisation of the violence towards his wife. The worker also makes it clear that she plans to talk to Con's wife about her current situation.

In this example, it is likely that the worker strongly disapproves of the offence which the client has committed and of the client's rationalisations for his behaviour. Nonetheless, consistent with pro-social modelling and reinforcement, the worker focuses on positives while at the same time making it clear that she does not approve of the offence and does not accept the rationalisations. She focuses on positives on the understanding that this is more likely to lead to changes in the client's behaviour than an approach which focuses on what the client has done wrong.

# Summary

Pro-social modelling and reinforcement is one of four key skills which comprise the evidence-based practice model presented in this book. The others are role clarification, problem-solving and relationship skills. Pro-social modelling and reinforcement involves four steps: identifying client pro-social comments and actions; rewarding those comments and actions; presenting oneself as a pro-social model; and challenging anti-social or pro-criminal comments and actions.

Pro-social modelling and reinforcement has a number of advantages. Its greatest advantage is that numerous research studies have pointed to its effectiveness in improving client outcomes. Nevertheless, a number of criticisms are sometimes made of this approach. These include that clients may say pro-social things but not do them; workers use this approach anyway; and that the approach is superficial, manipulative, judgmental and does not focus on client goals. Each of these criticisms is addressed in this chapter. How the approach fits with some different perspectives from feminist and critical theories to work across cultures is also discussed.

# 5 PROBLEM-SOLVING

Problem-solving approaches have been popular in the human services for many years. Perhaps the first person to popularise problem-solving in welfare settings was Helen Harris Perlman, in her book *Social Casework: A Problem Solving Process*, published in 1957. William Reid and Laura Epstein published *Task-centred Casework* in 1972, which again outlined a problem-solving model for casework practice. These models have since been refined further (e.g. Reid and Epstein 1972; Doel and Marsh 1992; Reid 1992; Marsh 2004). Most current social work and welfare texts continue to include material on problem-solving approaches (e.g. Hepworth, Rooney and Larson 2002; Compton and Galaway 2005).

The problem-solving model presented in this chapter makes use of much of the material presented in these publications. However, it relates this material specifically to work with involuntary clients. It also attempts to integrate principles of assessment, case planning and case management into the problem-solving framework. The model incorporates the principles related to effective outcomes in work with involuntary clients referred to in Chapter 2. The model has been tested and further developed in my research in probation and child protection (Trotter 1996a, 2004).

# Steps in the problem-solving process

The model includes seven steps: (1) problem survey; (2) problem ranking; (3) problem exploration; (4) setting goals; (5) developing a contract; (6) developing strategies and tasks; and (7) ongoing review.

It should be stated at the outset that, while workers are encouraged to work through the steps of the model as systematically as possible, in many instances this is not possible. In work with many involuntary clients—particularly those with drug-abuse problems, psychiatric illness or intellectual disability—working sequentially may be difficult. People's problems, or their perceptions of them, may change from one week to the next, or in some instances from one minute to the next. So in practice workers might find they move back and forth in relation to the various stages of the model. It is important, nonetheless, that the model is used to provide a clear structure for the interaction between the worker and client, and that the worker tries to work through the model sequentially, as far as possible.

The client should be given information about the nature of the problem-solving process. As mentioned earlier, some of the workers in child protection and probation with whom I have worked have the steps of the problem-solving process displayed in large print on a poster on their office wall. They are then able to show this to their clients, explain it to them, and regularly identify the stage they are at in relation to the process. This is certainly an approach I favour because it facilitates an open partnership approach. An example of the charts which workers have used is included as an Appendix to this book.

## Problem survey

The problem survey, the first step in the problem-solving process, begins after the initial role clarification. Its purpose is to gain a picture of the client's perception of the situation and the issues of concern to them. It sets the stage for further ongoing work with clients in relation to their problems.

## What is involved in the problem survey?

Clients are asked to list or identify any problems they may have. The worker might ask the client to identify anything in their life which they would like to change. The use of questions similar to those used in solution-focused counselling (e.g. Berg and De Jong 1996) may help to identify problems—for example, 'What would be different if everything was the way you wanted it to be?'

The aim is to get a written list of things the client is unhappy about or would like to change. In developing this list, the worker might work through an assessment framework or a risk assessment profile, which may be in use in their particular organisation. The way in which risk assessment frameworks can be integrated with the problem survey is discussed later in this chapter. If no such framework is available, the worker should prompt the client to talk about issues which might be problems—for example, employment, housing, family situation, drug use, recreation and finances.

The list should be written down on a white board or piece of paper, and should be viewed as the *client's* list of issues. The client is therefore the final arbiter of what is included on the list and what is not. The worker should, however, encourage the client to identify problems which the worker feels are related to the behaviour which has led the client to become a client.

As the client identifies different problems, the worker should ask the client to talk about each problem. Why is it a problem? How severe is the problem? How long has it been going on? For example, in relation to a problem of unemployment, the worker might seek to clarify with the client how long they have been unemployed; how they feel about this; whether they have worked previously; and how they fill in their days.

It may be appropriate to break a problem down, or partialise the problem. For example, a client may say they are depressed and the worker may seek to partialise different aspects of this problem. Is the depression related to specifics like accommodation or lack of relationships? Does it involve an inability to get out of bed in the mornings? Is the client suicidal?

It is important that the problems are listed in the client's terms and in the client's language. If the client has a problem with 'no work' or a 'very small apartment', the problem should be written in these terms rather than as 'unemployment' and 'inadequate accommodation'. The worker may rephrase problem definitions in order to be clear about what is being said. For example, the worker might say, 'You mean this apartment is not big enough for you and two children'. However, the problem list should as far as possible be the client's expression of the problem in the client's words.

As discussed later in this chapter, problem-solving approaches are sometimes criticised because of the focus on problems rather than strengths. Steve DeShazer (1988), in his work on solution-focused approaches, refers to 'complaints' rather than 'problems'. Dorothy Scott and Di O'Neill (1996), in their work on solution-focused approaches in child protection, refer to 'issues which currently concern the family'. I argue later that problem-solving is not a negative experience for clients; nonetheless, referring to problems as issues or things the client would like to change may help to make the problem survey less negative and less overwhelming for the client.

## Problem ranking

Once the problem survey has been completed—in other words, once the worker and the client have developed a list of problems or issues from the client's perspective—a decision should be made about which problems to work on. Generally it is appropriate to start with one, or perhaps two, manageable issues.

In work with involuntary clients, there are a number of guidelines for deciding with the client which issues need to be worked on. To begin with, there will sometimes be crisis situations which need immediate action, often before the worker has had time to work through the problem survey or problem-ranking process. For example, there could be a crisis which requires the immediate placement of children, or immediate hospitalisation of a drug user or a mentally ill client. Obviously, these situations will take priority.

The next problem to work on must be one which the client agrees is a problem. The worker may suggest that a particular problem is a good one to start with and give the client reasons for this. However, it is vital that the client views the problem as a problem.

It is also best to start with problems which have a good chance of being resolved. Some immediate success at the beginning of the problem-solving process provides an incentive to both worker and client. For example, it may not be appropriate to start with a housing problem if the worker is aware of a severe housing shortage in the area. There may be more chance of success if the worker and the client decide to work on a problem relating to a client being housebound with her young children. It may be that the worker is familiar with good daycare for children, or it may be that the client has relatives who could assist.

If resources are available to help solve the problem, there is more chance of achieving short-term success. It is, of course, very helpful at this stage if the worker has a good working knowledge of relevant resources.

While it is vital that the problem to be worked on is a real problem from the client's perspective, the worker should encourage the client to work on problems which are related to the reason the client is a client. For example, an offender may wish to work on a problem relating to her relationship with a drug-using partner. The worker, however, might feel that the partner has a negative influence on the client and leads her to greater use of drugs. The worker might therefore encourage the client to work on a problem relating to her drug use rather than the problem with her relationship.

If the worker feels strongly that the problem the client has chosen is not the most appropriate one to work on, then it may be appropriate to suggest to the client that two problems be worked on simultaneously. The client and worker might agree, for example, to address both the drug problem and the relationship problem. Nevertheless, it remains vital that the client does view both problems as real problems.

The worker may also encourage the client to work on problems in a manner which is consistent with pro-social values. For example, a male client who has been a perpetrator of domestic violence may have a problem with what he perceives as his partner's lack of support. He may want his partner to carry out more tasks around the home and generally be more supportive of him. The worker may feel that working on such a problem would be supporting a patriarchal view on the client's part. In this instance, the worker would discourage the client from working on this problem.

Finally, the focus of this problem-solving model is on practical rather than intra-psychic issues. The research in relation to psycho-analytic approaches in work with involuntary clients is not positive (Alexander and Parsons 1973; Fischer 1973; Wood 1978; Rubin 1985; Videka Sherman 1988; Gough 1993; Andrews and Bonta 2003). When clients raise non-specific problems such as depression, low self-esteem, anxiety or guilt, for example, they should be broken down into more tangible concerns. A client who expresses concern about feeling bad about herself and having low self-esteem might be asked to talk about why she has low self-esteem. It might be possible to relate this to not having friends, not having work, feeling stigmatised by being on a court order, or feeling inadequate because she has no money. Rather than dealing with the non-specific issue of low self-esteem, the worker and the client might choose to work on one of these more specific problems.

From my own direct practice work, and from workshops I have conducted with practising professionals, it is apparent that there is considerable variation in the time it takes to work through the problem survey and problem-ranking stages of the problem-solving process. In some instances, it is possible to work through these steps in one or two interviews; in other cases, it may take longer. It is not uncommon to work through the problem survey over as many as five or six interviews, move on to the next stage of the process and still have to return to the problem survey stage weeks later.

For example, in one instance I worked through the various stages of the problem-solving process with a young probationer whom I believed was an alcoholic. Despite my attempts to raise the issue, he consistently refused to identify his drinking as a problem for him. We worked on a number of other issues, including his family relationships. On one occasion, after some months, as he was about to leave the office he commented that he was worried because he had been drinking too much and this was what got him into trouble last time. (Situations such as these have been euphemistically referred to as 'door knob therapy'— it takes place when the client feels safe with one hand on the door and about to leave.) We were then able to resume the interview and go back to the problem survey stage of the problem-solving process. The client then began to explore this issue and to develop some strategies to address his fears that he might reoffend.

## Problem exploration

Some problem exploration will already have occurred during the problem survey stage. Nonetheless, once the worker has decided which problem to work on, it can be helpful to do some more exploration of the problem and factors which might impact on it. In some cases, this problem exploration might lead to a different definition of the problem.

The client should be asked to talk about how the problem began, when it began, what factors are preventing its solution, whether attempts have been made to solve the problem, and how successful they have been.

For example, a probation officer might be working with a young probationer, and between them they have agreed to work on the problem of the probationer's lack of employment. The probation officer then begins to explore this issue. He would want to know how long the young person had been unemployed; if she had ever worked; if so in what type of work; how long she remained in the job; whether she left the job voluntarily or was asked to leave; what the specific circumstances of her leaving were; whether she is seeking other work, and if so, what type; whether she has been for interviews; whether she uses newspapers or word of mouth to find out about positions; what education or skills she has; how she presents for interviews, and so on.

Some of this material will have been covered in the problem survey stage; however, the aim at this stage of the process is to learn as much as possible about the problem and the surrounding issues. It could become evident as the problem is explored that other issues need to be addressed before it can be resolved. For example, a young person might be seeking work which requires some skill or training she does not have. The problem might need to be redefined as inadequate skills to find the type of work she wants. This might lead to an exploration of her skills and possible training opportunities.

Jerry Keissling (1982), in his work in probation, suggests that probation officers should spend as long as they feel they need to in the problem exploration stage, and then spend some more time. In other words, it is very important to gain an understanding of the problem and its context at this stage. For example, there may be little point working on a plan for seeking employment if the client lives in an isolated area with no access to transport. This means that in the midst of the problem exploration it might be necessary to return to the problem survey and problem-ranking stages of the process. The worker and the client might agree to work initially on the problem of geographical isolation rather than immediately addressing the problem of employment. The problem exploration stage would then begin for the second time.

When the worker is satisfied that they have a clear picture of the problem in its broad context, the worker and the client should attempt to define what exactly the client wants to happen. In other words, what are the client's goals?

## Setting goals

It was pointed out in Chapter 2 that agreement on goals between worker and client consistently emerges in the research as being related to positive outcomes with both voluntary and involuntary clients (Rubin 1985; Sheldon 1987; Videka Sherman 1988; Trotter 2004). The development of goals is about the worker and the client reaching agreement on what they are trying to achieve together.

The worker and client may well have different interpretations of the goals, and these differences can sometimes be subtle. It is important, therefore, that goals are defined in specific terms and as far as possible leave little scope for different interpretations. Thus it is important that the specific goals are written down and a copy is available to both the worker and the client.

Examples of goals include:

- for Melinda to find part-time employment in a sales position within six weeks;
- for Melinda to obtain new accommodation with at least two bedrooms which is within walking distance of the city centre, or which is less than ten minutes' walk from a train or bus which goes at least every 30 minutes to the city centre;
- for Melinda to have regular contact (at least once a week for 30 minutes) with another woman who lives in her area;
- for Ben (aged seven) to stop hitting his sister (aged five) within one week.

Some examples of goals which are not sufficiently specific and which might lead to uncertainty include:

- for Melinda to get a job;
- for Melinda to find new accommodation;
- for Melinda to make friends;
- for Ben to treat his sister better.

## Developing a contract

At this stage, after the problems have been identified through the problem survey, ranked, further explored and goals set, a written contract is developed with the purpose of summarising these steps for the benefit of the worker and the client. Ideally the contract, as a summary of client problems and goals, should be written by the client. In practice, however, contracts are most often written by the worker in collaboration with the client. See the box for an example of a contract.

## Problem-solving contract

### Problems

1. Melinda has no work.
2. Melinda's house is too small for her and two children.
3. Melinda has no friends.
4. Melinda is worried about the violent behaviour of Ben (seven years) towards his sister Maeve (five years).

Initially it is agreed to work on the third and fourth problems.

### Goals

1. For Melinda to have regular contact (at least once a week for 30 minutes) with another woman who lives in her area.
2. For Ben to stop hitting his sister within one week.

### Other agreements (or ground rules)

1. For the worker to visit twice a week for the next month on Tuesday and Thursday mornings.
2. For the worker to ring before she visits so Melinda knows when to expect her.
3. For Melinda to be available for all visits.
4. For the two children to be home at least every second visit (on Thursdays).

## Developing strategies and tasks

The next step in the problem-solving process is the development of tasks or strategies to achieve the goals. This is sometimes referred to as 'developing solutions'.

There is often confusion about what is a task or strategy or solution and what is a goal. Certainly different writers have different definitions of goals and tasks. In simple terms, a *goal* is *what the client wishes to achieve*, and a *task* or *strategy* or *solution* is a *means of achieving it*. Finding new accommodation is a goal, whereas looking in the paper and visiting the department of housing are tasks to achieve that goal.

There are as many tasks available to workers as there are problems. William Reid (1985), in his work on family problem-solving, refers to session tasks—those carried out within the interview setting; home tasks—those carried out by the clients between sessions; and environmental tasks—which involve liaison with other agencies such as schools or courts. Environmental tasks may be carried out by the worker, the client, other professionals or others within the client's family or social networks.

Once a goal has been identified, the worker and the client discuss what can be done to achieve the goal. It is again important that the tasks, strategies or solutions developed to achieve the goals are developed by the client—or at least agreed to by the client.

In developing tasks, some discussion may take place about what has been tried previously and there may be some overlap with the problem exploration stage. To some extent, this overlap is unavoidable. The important thing is that the client and worker are clear about the nature of the problem and what the client hopes to achieve, and that methods to achieve this are developed.

Tasks, like goals, should be specific and clear. It should be a simple matter to identify whether or not a task has been carried out. A range of tasks might be carried out within an interview setting. In relation to the goal of employment, for example, tasks might include doing role plays of interviews; working through the newspapers or a website with a client looking for suitable work; discussing with the client different types of work and how suitable they might be; or examining the reasons why previous jobs have not been satisfactory.

Taking an example from probation, a client may be concerned about meeting her unpaid community work commitments; she might therefore identify a goal of getting through the community work hours.

Tasks undertaken in the interview might include the worker and client discussing transport arrangements, considering possible alternative community work placements and examining the work commitments of the client.

Taking a situation in child protection where a parent is having difficulty with a child who has temper tantrums, a worker might help the client to identify the circumstances in which the temper tantrums occur. A task to be undertaken within sessions might be to help the mother or father identify what factors might be bringing on the temper tantrums and how these factors could be modified.

Tasks carried out between sessions could include a young person going through the newspaper looking for possible jobs, or a parent trying out strategies to modify the circumstances which lead to a child's temper tantrums. They could involve getting information from the public transport authority about routes and timetables, or getting information about drug rehabilitation centres. They could include a parent taking a child out for a particular activity, or an adolescent phoning her mother.

Tasks or strategies which might be carried out by the worker include tasks involving advocacy on behalf of a client. This might entail the worker approaching schools, social security, courts or other organisations on behalf of the client. Alternatively, it might involve helping the client to write letters to those organisations.

Tasks might also include referral to other agencies—for example, for clients to attend ongoing courses or treatment groups, such as an anger management course, a sex offenders' group, a women's group, a families first program, a parenting skills course or a drug treatment program. Such tasks might include shorter-term referrals, such as the client visiting social security, visiting a housing worker, visiting an employment service or making an appointment to see a financial counsellor. In fact, referral to other agencies for particular services is more and more common in work with involuntary clients, as the principles of case management become more prevalent.

It is important, as William Reid (1997b) points out, that potential obstacles to task completion are examined. For example, in relation to the task of gathering information about work which is available, the worker might discuss with the client potential obstacles like the cost and method of getting to the employment service or accessing local papers. If, for example, the client has a literacy problem, the task may have to be restructured to accommodate this.

## Referrals

Making referrals is an important part of work with involuntary clients. It was argued in Chapter 2 that the referral process can be a key factor in achieving positive outcomes for clients. Outlined below are some general principles which can be applied when making referrals.

The referral should, wherever possible, be a part of the problem-solving process. In other words, it should follow the problem survey, problem ranking, problem exploration and goal-setting. The referral should preferably be suggested by the client, or at least agreed to by the client.

The client should make the initial contact where this is appropriate. There is a good argument for encouraging the client to take as much responsibility as possible for all aspects of the problem-solving process. This is consistent with the idea that clients are learning a process to help solve their own problems, a process which might prove to be useful at a later time.

It may be important, however, that the worker also makes contact with the referral agency. The worker should have information about whether referrals are followed up by clients and whether clients have found the referral helpful. The worker should also be satisfied that the agency provides a service which meets the client's needs.

In making referrals, workers should have knowledge about how long the client might have to wait for an appointment. Our child protection study (Trotter 2004) found that workers often did not follow up on referrals, and almost 20 per cent of the clients did not even attend one appointment at the agency to which they were referred. Certainly the clients are more likely to get to the referral agency if the referral is followed up by the worker within a few days.

As discussed in Chapter 2, there has been much criticism of case management. Certainly little is likely to be gained by referrals in urgent cases to programs with limited resources and long waiting lists. It may be better in these situations for direct practice workers to do some short-term problem-solving themselves, even if this can be done over only one or two sessions.

How much a worker should be expected to know about an agency to which referrals are made is a complex issue. Do you simply trust fellow professionals? Or, as a worker who supports evidence-based practice, do you examine the nature of the service being offered by other agencies?

One particular dilemma I faced in my work in probation related to referrals to a particular drug rehabilitation centre. The centre was eventually the subject of a government inquiry into misuse of drugs which had led to the deaths of a number of patients. Prior to this time, however, probation officers had received glossy brochures about the centre's program, and many had made referrals to it. It was only subsequently that we thought about the potential risks involved in referring clients to organisations with which we were not familiar.

If programs do not appear to be consistent with the research about what works, then referral to those groups is not appropriate. In fact, the evidence seems clear that some welfare programs are harmful, and it seems hard to justify an approach which simply trusts fellow workers to do the right thing. For example, a probation officer should exercise care in referring a young offender to a 'scared straight' or 'day-in-gaol' program, given the lack of research support for such programs (Lipsey 1991; Gendreau 1996; Andrews and Bonta 2003). Unfortunately the welfare field has seen too many programs which do not have an empirical base and are potentially harmful (Trotter 1996b).

## Groupwork

The focus of this book is on direct practice with individual clients and with families. Groupwork is outside its scope. Nonetheless, in developing tasks, workers often refer to group programs and some comment about the use of groups is appropriate. This is particularly so given the increasing popularity of groupwork in corrections settings. In fact, Maurice Vanstone (2004) suggests that structured groupwork programs in the probation field in the United Kingdom may be overwhelming individual work and threatening the collaborative practice model.

The groupwork programs which have proliferated in probation and prison settings in recent years are for the most part based on cognitive behavioural models. These programs, in the words of Peter Raynor (2003:79), 'put together a series of planned and sequential learning opportunities into a cumulative sequence covering an appropriate curriculum of skills and allowing plenty of opportunity to reinforce learning through structured practice'. (The reader is referred to the Cognitive Centre Foundation website in the United Kingdom, cognitivecentre.com, for descriptions of a range of structured programs based on what works and cognitive behavioural principles.) Research on these programs has shown promising results (Raynor and Vanstone 1996; Andrews 2001; Pearson et al. 2002), and probation officers, child protection workers and others who work with involuntary clients often work either directly or indirectly with them.

When is groupwork rather than individual work appropriate with clients? As I mentioned in Chapter 2, there is no doubt that groupwork can be effective with a range of involuntary clients. Whether group-work is preferable to individual work is a more difficult question to answer, however. Our state of knowledge about this issue is limited.

That said, groups can provide a source of support to their members, they can be influential in changing attitudes and they may provide an economical way of dealing with a large client caseload. On the other hand, as discussed in Chapter 2, peer group association which occurs in groups can sometimes lead to negative outcomes. There is some evidence of this in probation (Trotter 1995a), and also to some extent in mental health (Videka Sherman 1988).

It does appear that effective groups are generally characterised by the same effective practices that characterise work with individuals (Ferguson 1983; Videka Sherman 1988; Milgram and Rubin 1992; Andrews and Bonta 2003). In making decisions about whether individual work or groupwork is most appropriate, workers should consider the extent to which programs are consistent with the principles of effective practice.

## Ongoing review

The point has already been made that the problem-solving process must be used flexibly. The worker and client could be in the middle of developing goals or working through strategies in relation to a particular issue when it becomes evident that another problem should take precedence. It could be that the client has been in denial until that time about a problem, or a new problem may emerge. In these cases, it may be appropriate to return to the problem survey and problem-ranking stages, effectively starting the problem-solving process again.

Nevertheless, as I have said, the worker should attempt to ensure that the intervention does follow the problem-solving steps as far as possible. It is the responsibility of the worker to provide the structure, to give the client information about how the structure works, and to use the structure flexibly. As suggested earlier, having the structure displayed for clients to see can facilitate this (see Appendix).

The worker and client should regularly review how they are going in relation to the model as a whole, and to the individual steps. A regular review of identification of problems, performance of tasks and movement toward goals should take place. This can be linked with ongoing evaluation, as discussed in Chapter 8.

# Problem-solving, risk assessment and case planning

Workers with involuntary clients often have a dual purpose: to investigate and gather information about their clients for official decision-making purposes; and to help those clients with their problems. How does the problem-solving process relate to the assessment and case planning processes?

# Risk assessment and investigation

As indicated above, the problem survey ideally begins in the first interview, following some discussion about the role of the worker. The nature of the first interview varies according to the particular setting. In child protection, workers often have their first contact following an allegation of child abuse. The worker—or more often two workers—will generally visit the family in their home in order to investigate the allegations and offer assistance. First contacts in probation sometimes occur at court, either before or after the client has been sentenced. First contacts in mental health sometimes occur at a hospital or following an after-hours call from police. In a school setting, they might occur immediately following an outburst in the classroom.

In other words, first contacts often occur at a time of crisis. In these instances, the workers will initially need to deal with the crisis at hand. This may involve making some immediate decisions, such as the removal of a child or hospitalisation.

In other cases, the first contact between a worker and a client may occur after a court case and sentencing have been completed, after a case of child abuse has been substantiated, or after a mental health patient has been released from hospital. In these instances, the worker and client are more likely to have time to work through an assessment process without the pressure of having to make crisis-dictated decisions.

In such cases, the worker is often asked to work through a specific risk-assessment format. As discussed in Chapter 2, formalised risk-assessment profiles, frameworks or screening devices are increasingly used in work with involuntary clients—particularly in corrections, child protection and mental health (see Schwalbe 2004 for a discussion about various risk-assessment tools).

There are good reasons for using formalised risk-assessment profiles. First, the evidence suggests that formalised risk assessments are more accurate than clinical or professional judgments (e.g. Schwalbe 2004). A number of studies with different types of client groups have compared risk assessments undertaken by professionals relying on clinical or professional judgment with risk assessments undertaken using risk-assessment profiles. The workers using the profiles generally predict the future behaviour of clients (for example, further offending, child abuse, suicide) more accurately than those using clinical judgment alone (Schwalbe 2004).

There are also some very good reasons for targeting high-risk clients. There is evidence that clients in the correctional system benefit more from services if they are high-risk. Low-risk clients tend not to reoffend anyway, and may be harmed by intensive services (Andrews and Bonta 2003). Similarly, in work with other involuntary clients, it makes sense to target scarce resources towards those with the most problems.

There are many risk-assessment profiles available. In the corrections field, for example, there are profiles which predict reoffending among general populations of offenders and profiles which predict reoffending among specific groups such as sex offenders, violent offenders or young offenders. The profiles may aim simply to predict risk, or they may also aim to provide information about needs, which in turn may assist in developing intervention strategies.

What do risk-assessment profiles look like? One example is the 'Level of Service Inventory—Revised', which is used in many probation services in Canada, the United States, the United Kingdom and Australia (Andrews and Bonta 2003). It contains a checklist of items including criminal history, education, employment, finances, family, accommodation, leisure, companions, alcohol and drug use, emotional issues and attitudes. Each of the items is broken down into sub-items, such as age at first offence, dissatisfaction with marital situation, or criminal acquaintances. The maximum score is 54, with offenders classified as high-, medium- or low-risk depending on their score.

In gathering information to complete the profile, the worker interviews the client and also collects information from other sources. For example, a probation officer may have information on file such as a police report and prior offences. The probation officer may also talk to an offender's parents or spouse as part of the assessment process. In addition, they may talk to previous probation officers or other welfare professionals who have been involved with the probationer.

Child protection and mental health risk assessments tend to be less dependent on numerical scores, but nevertheless require workers to work through a checklist of factors in a similar way to the corrections risk assessments (Holder and Salovitz 2001; Schwalbe 2004).

I pointed out in Chapter 2 that, despite the apparent superiority of risk-assessment profiles over clinical or professional assessments, and despite the arguments in favour of focusing on high-risk clients, formalised risk-assessment processes are often criticised.

What is the basis of these criticisms? First, it is argued that the focus on risk can be at the expense of treatment. For example, a study of case planning meetings in the United Kingdom suggested that only about 15 per cent of the discussion in meetings was about treatment, the remainder focusing largely on risk assessment (Farmer 1999). Second, risk assessments are often done in a hurry and not completed as intended. Third, it is argued that risk assessments target socially and economically disadvantaged clients, and are therefore unfair. For example, clients without family support, employment or ongoing accommodation will be more likely to be assessed as high-risk. And fourth, risk-assessment profiles are criticised because workers often disregard them when making decisions about services—they often prefer to rely on their own clinical or professional judgment (Schwalbe 2004).

Certainly there are arguments both for and against the use of risk-assessment profiles. What is clear, however, is that they are increasingly being used in work with involuntary clients (Robinson 2003; Schwalbe 2004). The question therefore arises of how they can be used to provide more effective services to those clients and how they can be integrated into the problem-solving process.

## Integrating risk assessment and problem-solving

At first glance, this appears problematic. It has been emphasised throughout this book that workers should work with the client's view of the problem. Yet risk assessment involves the worker collecting accurate information from the worker's perspective.

Chapter 3 discussed the complexity of the worker's dual social control/helping role. As emphasised there, workers should talk to clients about their role and should be specific about the purpose of the intervention. The reason for gathering information should be clear to the client. Is it being gathered as part of a problem-solving process or for the purpose of making decisions about the client (e.g. allocation to an intensive supervision program, removal of a child, hospitalisation or expulsion from school)? Or is it a combination of these things? This discussion is part of the role-clarification process. The intervention is likely to be more successful if the client can see the parallel risk assessment and problem survey processes as part of the worker's social control/helping role.

As the worker works through the risk-assessment format, they can ask the client to identify the issues which the client sees as problems. The risk-assessment profiles lend themselves to this process as they contain checklists of potential issues, which the worker would work through normally in the problem survey process. In completing the risk assessment the worker and client can thereby develop the list of problems which the client would like to address. This list can be developed separately from the risk-assessment documentation, or it can be included in the risk-assessment documentation and summarised in writing for the benefit of the client towards the end of the assessment.

Another way of dealing with the need to both assess risk and work with the client's view of the problem is to develop two problem lists— one a problem list developed through the problem survey process described above, and the other a list of problems as defined by the worker during the risk assessment process. Such an approach allows for the investigatory nature of the work to be carried out while at the same time recognising the importance of working with client definitions of problems if change is to be achieved. This can lead in turn to the definition of negotiable and non-negotiable problems and issues, as discussed below.

The issue of different problem definitions between the worker and the client is discussed again later in this chapter.

# How does the problem-solving contract relate to a case plan?

In Chapter 1, a distinction was made between problem-solving and case planning. Problem-solving involves counselling or therapeutic work with clients, whereas case planning involves the development of longer-term plans, often including the use of community resources.

As discussed in Chapter 1, the distinction between case planning and problem-solving is often unclear. There is a degree of overlap between them. Case planning is conceptualised in this book as relating to non-negotiable aspects of the direct practice intervention. A case plan can be conceptualised as the 'bottom line', or what the worker or a court requires of the client. (Case management, on the other hand, involves the ongoing oversight and monitoring of the case plan.)

In Chapter 1, these concepts were illustrated with an example from child protection. The following example explores these concepts further. A child is placed on a court order following an investigation by child protection workers regarding neglect by her parents. A case plan is developed by the worker in consultation with the client, the client's family, other professionals and other workers in the organisation. The case plan is ratified by a formal case-planning meeting. The case plan may be based on the risk assessment which will have been undertaken either before or after the court hearing.

The case plan involves the child being placed with relatives for a period of three months, with a view to further assessment of the parents' situation. As part of the case plan, the parents are asked to maintain regular contact with the child, and the worker is to regularly monitor the contact between the parents and the child. A further case-planning meeting is scheduled in three months to decide whether or not the child is to be returned to the parents.

The family may have been consulted about this case plan; however, they may not agree with it. The parents may believe that the child should be returned to live with them immediately. The case plan is, however, non-negotiable—or at least can only be changed by the worker. It constitutes a set of requirements or expectations alongside which the problem-solving process may take place.

The worker then oversees or manages the case plan and works through the problem-solving process with the parents (and the child if the child is old enough). The parents might identify having their child returned to them after three months as a goal, and the problem-solving process and contract would then focus on this issue. Nonetheless, the three-month period during which the child is to be placed away from home is non-negotiable.

Similar examples can be drawn from work with other groups of involuntary clients. In probation, a case plan might include non-negotiable areas relating to the court order, such as requirements for completing community work or attending for drug treatment. The problem-solving process and contract might, however, focus on goals relating to employment or becoming drug-free.

As discussed in Chapter 3, effective work with involuntary clients involves being clear about what is negotiable and what is not negotiable. The problem-solving process, as it is conceptualised in this book, involves working with issues which are negotiable and being clear about what is negotiable and what is not.

# Criticisms of a problem-solving approach

A number of criticisms have been levelled at problem-solving approaches. Outlined below is my attempt to address some of these criticisms, as well as some of the difficulties which workers often experience using the problem-solving framework.

## Problem-solving is too negative

Problem-solving approaches are sometimes criticised as being negative, and focusing on weaknesses rather than strengths. Listing all the things which are wrong in someone's life and working out which one most needs attention could lead someone to a state of despair. A number of writers have pointed to the value of focusing on strengths rather than problems (e.g. Saleebey 2001). Solution-focused and narrative approaches are often favoured because they focus on strengths rather than problem-focused approaches (e.g. DeShazer 1988; White and Epston 1989). It is argued that the focus should be on times when things have gone well for the client and on exceptions to the problem rather than the problem itself. Others argue in favour of a focus on resilience, or the client's ability to cope with stressful experiences and environments, rather than a focus on problems (Allison et al. 2003).

The working model presented in this book, however, focuses very strongly on strengths and successes through the pro-social approach. It focuses on small steps with a high chance of success in the development of tasks, and it includes the purposeful use of an optimistic approach (detailed in Chapter 6).

The assessment process, with its inevitable focus on problems, is a necessary part of work with most involuntary clients. Nonetheless, problem-solving, accompanied by the other aspects of the intervention model presented in this book, aims to make the direct practice experience overall a positive one.

Perhaps the best counter to the argument that problem-solving is too negative lies in the considerable body of research over several decades which suggests that accurately defining problems or issues in client terms is related to improved outcomes (Reid and Hanrahan 1982; Rubin 1985; Sheldon 1987; Videka Sherman 1988; Jones and Alcabes 1993; Trotter 1996a; Reid 1997b; Andrews and Bonta 2003; Trotter 2004).

## What if clients say they have no problems?

How do you use a problem-solving framework when clients insist that they have no problems? In child protection, for example, a parent or an adolescent might say that everything is fine, the situation has been misinterpreted or misjudged, and there is no need to do any work with them. Probationers, similarly, will sometimes express the view that they accept the need to report as required but that they do not want assistance with any issues.

Involuntary clients have a choice to accept or refuse the helping or counselling services offered to them. Clients can legally be required to receive some services; however, they cannot be forced to work through a problem-solving process in any meaningful way. Jones and Alcabes (1993) argue that clients do not become clients until they reach agreement with the worker about the goals of the intervention. Prior to this time, they argue, the worker is simply working towards helping the client to become a client—in other words, towards encouraging the client to accept the offer of helping services.

If clients choose not to identify issues to work on, then the worker has little choice but to focus on issues of role clarification, to make use of the principles of pro-social modelling and relationship skills, and to hope that the client will choose to utilise more therapeutic services at a later time. The worker might continue to explain to the client that they would like to help with issues of concern to them, that this has been very helpful with other clients, and that this is part of their job. The worker might offer to work on non-threatening issues with the client—income security benefits, for example. In the long run, however, working through a problem-solving process requires the client to invest some level of trust in the worker. This trust can take time to develop, and might in fact never develop—at least with that particular worker.

## Problem-solving does not focus on the real problem

It is sometimes argued that problem-solving approaches do not focus on the 'real' problem because of the focus on the problem as the client defines it. Critics taking this line argue that clients often do not understand, or even acknowledge, their own problems. For example, a client may have perpetrated sexual abuse against a child and continue to believe that the child was not harmed by the incident and that they did nothing wrong. Working with the client's definition of the problem may have the worker and the client working towards improving the client's housing or marital relationship rather than focusing on the real problem—that of sexual abuse.

In such instances, the worker should encourage the client to identify the real problems as problems. The worker might say to the client, 'It seems to me that your sexual interest in young children has got you into all sorts of trouble in the past. I think we should include this on the list.' However, if the client continues to be unwilling to accept that this is a problem for him, then it should not be included in the problem survey. The worker might raise the issue again in subsequent interviews; however, until the client agrees, it should not be included on the list.

This is not to say that the worker should ignore problems which the worker sees but the client doesn't. On the contrary, through using pro-social skills, the worker should simultaneously encourage the pro-social actions and behaviours of the client, challenge rationalisations and encourage the client to look at problems from different perspectives. There may also be non-negotiable requirements which the client must fulfil that address the 'real' problem. For example, the client might be required to seek treatment for sexual problems or to refrain from mixing with young people.

Reference was made earlier to the idea of developing two problem lists—one a list of client problems and the other a list of problems, or risk factors, as they are perceived by the worker. Some participants in my workshops have found this useful in situations where there is disagreement between the worker and client about the nature of the client's problems. It is important, as suggested in Chapter 4, that the worker is explicit about the things that they believe the client should change, and lists of problems for both worker and client can be an appropriate method of doing this.

While the worker may aim to encourage the client to recognise the 'real' problem, and work with two problem lists, it remains crucial that the problems which are subsequently dealt with are viewed by the client as problems. Change in relation to the 'real' problem is only likely to occur after the client accepts that the problem is real.

The collaborative problem-solving model, accompanied by pro-social modelling, a focus on role clarification and appropriate use of the relationship, was effective with high-risk probationers and high-risk protection clients in my studies. Many of those clients were in a state of denial (Trotter 1996a, 2004). Despite the apparent difficulties, it appears to be the most appropriate way of working with involuntary clients. A more directive approach, which defines the problem and sets tasks for, rather than with, the client is less likely to be successful (see Chapter 2).

## What about clients who don't follow through as arranged?

Involuntary clients will sometimes work through the problem-solving process in the interview situation and agree to undertake tasks between interviews; however, when they return for the next interview, they will not have done so. In these circumstances, the worker should discuss with the client why the task has not been performed. Was the task actually agreed to by the client? Or was the task developed by the worker, with the client agreeing only reluctantly? Was the task too difficult? Did the task lack meaning for the client? Was the problem relating to the task not a priority for the client, or has it changed in some way? Were obstacles to carrying out the task not identified prior to the task being set? It is important that failure to perform tasks is not viewed as a failure on the part of the client. A task which is not performed is an unsatisfactory task and needs to be revised.

Reference was made earlier to William Reid's (1997b) review of research on task-centred practice, in which he points to the importance of preparing clients to undertake tasks. He suggests that tasks are more likely to be completed if clients are offered incentives to complete the task, if potential obstacles are examined and if the task is rehearsed. As discussed earlier, simply assigning a task as a directive is less likely to lead to its successful completion.

# How can you use a problem-solving process with intellectually disabled, psychiatrically ill or drug-addicted clients?

Involuntary clients often have multiple issues. A probationer, for example, may have brain damage, intellectual disability, drug addiction and/or mental health problems. It can be very difficult to work through a problem-solving process with a client who cannot remember from week to week, or day to day, what has been decided—or who consistently misinterprets or misunderstands the worker's meaning.

The research cited in Chapter 2, with mentally ill, intellectually disabled and drug-addicted clients, suggests that working with client definitions of problems and client goals is important to positive outcomes with these groups of clients. This was certainly confirmed in my studies, which found that clients with drug addictions, mental health issues and limited intellectual ability responded to workers with effective practice skills (Trotter 1996a, 2004).

In work with this group of clients, it seems that the best method is simply to persevere. While it may be appropriate to be directive in relation to the legal requirements of a court order, there is little value in directing clients to perform tasks as part of a problem-solving process. Such an approach is unlikely to be successful in terms of improving client outcomes. Despite the real difficulties which workers experience in working collaboratively with this client group, a willingness to persevere with a collaborative approach is likely to be of long-term benefit to the client.

A case example illustrates this point. A schizophrenic client had a long history of involuntary psychiatric hospital admissions relating to her consistent failure to take her prescribed medication. She would be released from hospital and usually readmitted within about three months. This usually occurred after having been picked up by the police because she was wandering on a busy road, walking around late at night with few clothes on, or for some other potentially self-destructive behaviour.

In working through the problem-solving process with this client following her discharge from hospital, it became apparent to the worker that the client did not see failing to take her medication as a problem. She in fact said that she did not like to take the medication because it meant that the voices would go away and she would be lonely. She actually felt happier without the medication.

The client did, however, define her frequent hospital admissions as a problem. The worker and the client then began to work on the problem as the client defined it, which led in turn to the development of strategies relating to the client's personal safety rather than focusing on her medication.

## Problem-solving supports the status quo

One further criticism of problem-solving is that it supports the status quo. In other words, it focuses on problems as defined by the client, which may not take into account broader perspectives. For example, in work with a male perpetrator of domestic violence, the client's definition of the problem is unlikely to incorporate broader issues of patriarchy and sexism.

Again, while the problem-solving approach may have a limited focus, in combination with the pro-social approach there is scope to encourage the client to see things from a different perspective. Using the domestic violence example, the worker may use pro-social skills to encourage and reward any comments which recognise the difficulties which women experience. The worker may confront patriarchal assumptions or sexist comments from the client. Further, feminist consciousness-raising might be used as a task or strategy to address a defined problem.

Critics who argue that problem-solving supports the status quo also point to its focus on individuals rather than systems. They suggest that system change rather than individual change is more likely to lead to long-term improvement in problems such as child abuse, crime, homelessness and violence. In response to this argument, I would reiterate the comments I made in Chapter 2. Direct work takes place with large numbers of involuntary clients around the world. The United States has millions of people in the criminal justice system alone. This is not to say that direct action to change political, social and economic systems is not of vital importance to this particular client group. It is simply to say that direct practice has an important place in welfare and corrections systems around the world. It is important that this work is done well.

## *Case example*

In this case example, a mother, Roslyn, has been leaving her two children aged three and five at home alone, sometimes for several hours. It is a similar situation to that described in the child protection case study in Chapter 3. This is the second visit by a child protection worker to the woman's home. The worker is beginning to work through the problem survey stage of the problem-solving process.

This interview is carried out by the child protection worker, but had the worker chosen to refer the family to a community agency, a similar interview might have been conducted by a worker from that agency.

*Worker:* Hi, Roslyn.

*Roslyn:* Hi.

*Worker:* How are you?

*Roslyn:* Oh, not bad, not bad.

*Worker:* I was saying last week that we could look at some of the issues that are worrying you at the moment. We could work through them and see if there is anything you can do or I can do, or we can do together, to help with these problems.

*Roslyn:* I've been thinking a bit about that. It is a bit of a worry with the kids. I need some time to myself, I need to be able to go out. There's some things you can't do with kids around.

*Worker:* I am going to start writing these things down—so I get a list of the issues. The first thing we could put on the list is about the kids.

*Roslyn:* I need to be able to get out sometimes without the kids.

*Worker:* So will I write down getting out without the kids?

*Roslyn:* Yes. I mean I'd like to be able to go out on a Saturday night sometimes, to get a bit of a social life. Maybe go shopping sometimes without the kids, so

I don't have to put up with them running riot in the supermarket and embarrassing me.

*Worker:* They embarrass you?

*Roslyn:* Yes. Last week Tom knocked a bottle off the shelf and it smashed all over the floor, and he was running all over the place. That's why I don't take them shopping with me, that's why I leave them at home.

*Worker:* We have talked about that, about leaving them at home, haven't we? And as I mentioned before, this is something that the department is not happy about—I am not happy about it either. However, I can see the problem that you've got with taking them to the supermarket. I know what kids can be like in supermarkets.

*Roslyn:* Yes, they are terrible.

*Worker:* So doing the shopping with the kids, that is a problem. You need either to be able to do it without the kids or manage to keep them under control when they are with you. [Showing the notes to the client] I have written down the problem of you getting out, having some independence and also the problem with taking Tom to the supermarket.

*Roslyn:* Yes, it's two things. Getting out and having some independence, having some time to myself. But it would be nice if I could take Tom somewhere where he didn't go wild, where he didn't just run all over the place like that. He is often like that at home as well. He just doesn't respect me—just like his father.

*Worker:* Can you tell me about his father? Does he ever see the children?

*Roslyn:* He left three years ago, after Tom was born, and I haven't seen him since. I have no idea where he is.

*Worker:* And you have had to raise the children on your own?

*Roslyn:* Yes.

*Worker:* It seems very unfair. So tell me more about Tom's behaviour. Does he have a bad temper?

*Roslyn:* Oh, well he has got a temper but the problem is that he is just out of control. I say 'No' and he just doesn't listen.

*Worker:* So he doesn't take any notice of you? He won't do what you're telling him?

*Roslyn:* No. I can tell him to be quiet, not to run around but off he goes and it's like I have not spoken.

*Worker:* How does he get on with his sister?

*Roslyn:* They fight all the time. You know, she's playing quietly with something and then along he comes and starts interfering and then she's screaming and hitting him and it gets so frustrating.

*Worker:* Does he hurt her?

*Roslyn:* Not yet, but as he gets bigger I think he might. Now it's really just annoying.

*Worker:* It must be frustrating.

*Roslyn:* I don't feel like having anyone to the house. If I did make some new friends, I wouldn't want to bring them home with the kids running riot like that.

*Worker:* You would also like to be able to have people at home sometimes without the kids performing? Is that something else we could add to this list?

*Roslyn:* Yes. I need to be able to get out a bit or have people over or something.

*Worker:* I'm not saying that I can solve these problems for you; however, if we sort out just what is worrying you, there may be something you can do or I can do, or that we can do together, to help the situation. This is the idea of my job. Obviously, you know, I have an issue with the kids being left. You know that, and I've explained that.

*Roslyn:* Yeah, I know, you told me last time. I know, I know, I can't do it or else we could have to go to court.

*Worker:* I am pleased to hear you say that. It sounds like you understand the situation. Anyway, it seems to me that the best way to ensure that the kids are not left at home is to deal with these other problems that you have got. So that is what I'm hoping to do.

*Roslyn:* Well, it sort of fixes both problems, doesn't it?

*Worker:* I hope so. What I would like to do is try to get a picture of all of the issues which are of concern to you and then pick one or two of them for a start and see what we can do about them.

*Roslyn:* OK.

*Worker:* I have used this method a lot before and also there's a lot written about this way of working. I have found that it is a very good way of working with people which actually gets you somewhere.

*Roslyn:* Well, it's better than someone just coming in and saying you have to do this and you are doing that wrong.

*Worker:* You seem to understand what I am saying. Your cooperation in this process is very helpful. I think it will help you and the children too.

*Roslyn:* Good. I hope so.

*Worker:* We were talking about these fights that they have. You were saying you get frustrated.

*Roslyn:* Oh yes. They will be watching TV and I'm trying to get dinner and Mandy starts doing something from school and Tom tries to get all over it. He pulls her pencils away and throws things around and she just gets really frustrated and then she gets mad with him. And he is tough. I mean he is only three but he is really strong for his age already. He hasn't hurt her yet but he will.

*Worker:* What have you tried to do about it?

*Roslyn:* Oh, I yell at them. I yell at them all the time. I smack them. I tell them not to do it. What more can I do? But it makes no difference.

*Worker:* Well, that sounds very irritating, frustrating.

In this example, the worker is attempting to get a written list of the issues which are of concern to Roslyn. Several issues are identified: getting out without the children; Tom's uncontrollable behaviour; the fighting between the two children; and not being able to invite anyone to the house. The worker makes use of the pro-social principles in emphasising the importance of not leaving the children unsupervised and in praising the client for her cooperation. The worker also talks about his role.

This example illustrates one segment of the problem survey. Once the worker is satisfied that the client has identified the major issues of concern, the worker and client will move on to the next stage of the problem-solving process, problem ranking.

# Summary

The problem-solving process involves seven steps: (1) problem survey; (2) problem ranking; (3) problem exploration; (4) setting goals; (5) developing a contract; (6) developing strategies and tasks; (7) ongoing review. The steps are used flexibly and the focus is on the client's definitions of problems and goals rather than the worker's definitions. The steps are used simultaneously with the pro-social approach, role clarification and an appropriate client–worker relationship.

Criticisms and questions sometimes expressed about the problem-solving approach include the following: problem-solving is too negative;

clients may say that they have no problems; clients may fail to follow through on tasks and strategies; some clients—particularly those with intellectual disability, drug addiction or psychiatric illness—may have difficulty participating in the process; the process may not address the real problem; and it promotes the status quo by working with individuals rather than systems.

Each of these difficulties and criticisms has been addressed; however, I have also stressed that it is important to persist with the problem-solving approach, along with role clarification, and pro-social modelling and reinforcement if successful outcomes are to be achieved. The client–worker relationship may also be an important factor, and this is discussed in the next chapter.

# 6 THE RELATIONSHIP

Chapter 2 highlighted different aspects of the client–worker relationship, including empathy, optimism, humour and self-disclosure. Some social work and welfare texts include other factors in discussions about the casework relationship—for example, the use of authority, confidentiality and genuineness. The focus on work with involuntary clients has led me to place discussion about these factors in other sections of the book. The use of authority is discussed as part of role clarification in Chapter 3 and as part of pro-social modelling and reinforcement in Chapter 4. The issue of confidentiality is discussed under role clarification in Chapter 3. Similarly, the issue of genuineness and openness is discussed in Chapters 3 and 4.

This chapter discusses empathy, optimism, humour and self-disclosure. It also includes a discussion about worker safety and dealing with violent clients.

# Empathy

Empathy is defined by Hogan (1969:307) as 'the intellectual or imaginative apprehension of another's condition or state of mind'. It involves a 'willingness to put oneself in another's place'. Empathy can be measured by the use of an empathy test or scale (see Trotter 1990).

*Reflective listening* is a practical manifestation of empathy. It involves a worker responding in an understanding manner to comments made by the client. It recognises both the feeling and content of the client's expressions. It also involves the worker physically attending to the client—making eye contact, for example. Andrews et al. (1979) found a positive correlation between the scores of probation officers on a scale of empathy and the same officers' use of reflective listening practices. In other words, empathic people tend to make use of reflective listening practices, and those making use of reflective listening practices tend to be empathic.

Chapter 2 pointed to research which suggests that, in work with involuntary clients, there is no clear relationship between worker effectiveness and scores on empathy scales or use of reflective listening practices. In other words, more empathic workers seem to do no better with their clients than less empathic workers.

On the other hand, there is some evidence (cited in Chapter 2) that empathic skills are valuable if accompanied by the use of other effective practice skills, such as the use of pro-social modelling, problem-solving and appropriate role clarification. Certainly the collaborative practice model promoted in this book assumes that workers have a capacity to understand the client's point of view. It was also evident in our child protection study that clients had better outcomes if they felt that their worker understood their point of view. It is appropriate, therefore, to consider the nature of empathy and reflective listening, and to explore how these skills can be integrated with other effective approaches.

What are reflective or empathic listening practices? Reflective listening involves paraphrasing the statements of another person. A lot of work was done on empathy and reflective listening in the 1960s and

1970s. At that time, client-centred counselling, with its focus on the relationship, was more popular than it is today. Robert Carkhuff (1969) and more recently Hepworth, Rooney and Larson (2002) have outlined scales for empathic understanding and communication. At level 1 on Carkhuff's scale, for example, the worker communicates no awareness of the client's feelings or expressions—in other words, is uninterested or operating from a 'pre-conceived frame of reference'. At level 5, the worker's responses 'add significantly to the feeling and meaning of the expressions' of the client (Carkhuff 1969:317). The worker is 'tuned in' to the client.

The following example sets out an example of a low-level empathic response (Worker 1), a medium-level empathic response (Worker 2) and a high-level empathic response (Worker 3).

## *Empathic responses*

*Client:* I am sick of this. I have no money. I can't pay the rent and I need a job. But there aren't any jobs anywhere. I am going to have to do something.

*Worker 1:* Don't worry. It's the same for everyone at the moment.

*Worker 2:* You just feel that everything is hopeless.

*Worker 3:* You sound like you are feeling pretty desperate. Lack of work and money are real problems.

The third comment responds to the client's feelings and to the meaning or content of the client's expressions.

In work with involuntary clients, the worker might make use of the pro-social approach and role clarification in response to this comment. If, for example, the client were a probationer who had a history of property offences the conversation might go something like this:

### *Empathic response to involuntary client*

*Client:* I am sick of this. I have no money. I can't pay the rent and I need a job. But there aren't any jobs anywhere. I am going to have to do something.

*Worker:* You sound like you're feeling pretty desperate. Lack of work and money are real problems. I am pleased that you have decided to tell me about this. I would like to help you sort things out if I can.

The worker is offering a verbal reward to the client for having raised the problem—a problem which is likely to relate to his offending behaviour. The worker is also making it clear that she perceives her role as being to help the client with problems such as these.

The differences between the empathic response alone and the response which incorporates empathy, role clarification and pro-social reinforcement may seem minimal. It does appear, however—as discussed in Chapter 2—that in work with involuntary clients the use of empathic comments alone in these situations can be unhelpful, particularly in response to client expressions which might be justifying or rationalising anti-social or criminal behaviour.

The following example from child protection involves a mother who has hit her two-year-old twins, resulting in them being admitted to hospital. The family was subsequently placed on a supervision order.

## *Empathic response in child protection*

*Mother:* The children are so naughty at the moment. I put them to bed for their afternoon sleep and they just lie there and scream. They drive me mad.

An empathic response might be:

*Worker:* You seem to be very frustrated. Kids are such hard work, aren't they?

A response which incorporated the principles of effective work with involuntary clients might be:

*Worker:* You sound very frustrated. I am pleased that you can talk to me about these feelings. I would really like to help you sort out some other ways of dealing with the kids. Was this how you felt when you hit the children last month?

This response acknowledges the client's feelings; it reinforces the fact that the client is talking about her feelings; it refers to the helping role of the worker; and it makes it clear that the worker believes alternatives need to be found for the anti-social behaviour of the client.

To respond to every client comment with responses which include each of the principles of effective work with involuntary clients is both impractical and undesirable. It is, however, important that the worker responds in a genuine manner and that the effective practice skills become part of the worker's natural style. These examples simply illustrate the skills which, in practice, might be used over a longer period.

## Touching

One issue which is sometimes raised by workers with involuntary clients—particularly those who work in residential settings—is the extent to which it is appropriate to use physical expressions of warmth towards clients.

Sometimes when clients are upset or distressed, their workers will touch or hug them. Certainly touch can be a powerful method of communicating feelings. Some workers say that it is important in the development of their relationships with clients and that they feel comfortable with it. It could be argued that appropriate physical contact with clients is part of pro-social modelling. Unfortunately, knowledge about the relative advantages and disadvantages of physical contact is very limited. While the topic is sometimes addressed in the helping literature, there is little agreement or research about when touch is appropriate and when it isn't (Strozier, Krizek and Sale 2003; Chestnut 2004). This is further complicated by the fact that different cultural groups often have different views about the appropriateness of physical contact.

Given this limited knowledge, it is not possible to offer any prescriptive guidelines. It is clear, however, that physical contact can be offensive, and male workers in particular should exercise great care in the use of physical contact with clients. When physical contact is part of the client–worker relationship, it should relate to the specific role the worker plays with the client. For example, some level of physical contact may be appropriate for residential workers who fulfil full-time carer roles, but is not likely to be appropriate for probation officers in the normal course of their duties.

# Optimism

It was argued in Chapter 2 that workers who are optimistic are more likely to help their clients—that worker optimism is one factor, amongst others, which relates to positive client outcomes. The concepts of 'hope' (that if workers are hopeful about their clients' prospects, their clients are likely to do better) and self-efficacy (that if clients expect to do well, they are more likely to do so) were also referred to.

An optimistic approach by workers is consistent with and facilitates the use of other skills. For example, in using pro-social skills, the worker focuses on the client's strengths and rewards positive comments and actions. In problem-solving, the worker aims for short-term successes in relation to achievable goals.

Involuntary clients, however, on the whole have little reason to feel optimistic. They have been judged by the community as being deviant in one way or another, and have been sanctioned by the community for this deviance. They are likely to feel stigmatised and in many cases pessimistic about the future. On top of this (as discussed in Chapter 2), workers are often pessimistic about their clients' prospects.

Yet in this context it is important that workers foster hope and optimism. How can workers be optimistic? What does this mean in day-to-day practice with involuntary clients?

Workers should believe in their capacity to help. A worker who is clear about the theoretical basis of their work and who is familiar with research about effectiveness can communicate their ability to help.

The worker might say to the client: 'I have made use of this approach with my clients in the past and they have found it very helpful. I think you will also find it helpful.' Or: 'I think I can help you sort out some of these problems.'

When clients present pessimistic interpretations of events, these should be challenged. Martin Seligman (1995) reports on the success of programs with depressed schoolchildren which taught them to challenge pessimistic interpretations of events. Similarly, solution-focused approaches (e.g. De Jong and Miller 1996) emphasise the importance of focusing on successes or exceptions in counselling work. Their proponents argue that the worker should focus on when things went well rather than when things went badly.

The following is an example of a positive interpretation of a client comment. The client says: 'My mother is a very bad-tempered woman and impossible to live with.' The worker responds: 'Do you mean that your mother was in a bad temper this morning? I thought you had been living with her for many years. Are there occasions when she is not in a bad temper?'

Or a client might comment: 'I could not go back to school. I failed everything when I was there.' This might attract a response from the worker such as: 'I understand from your school report on the file that you passed one subject in the last year at school but that you did little work. It seems to me that you might well have the ability to do well at school.'

The use of optimism can also help clients to see their situation in its social and political context. Take, for example, a single mother with four children who feels that she will never be able to give her children the things she would like them to have. The worker might try to help the woman understand that she is not to blame for her situation, that there are many women in a similar position to her and that she can still be a good mother despite her disadvantages.

Pessimistic thinking might be identified as a problem for a client through the problem-solving process. The worker might then be able to help the client work through strategies for dealing with negative thinking. Martin Seligman (1990, 1995) outlines a number of strategies developed from his research in this area—including learning to argue with your own pessimistic thinking; looking for alternative explanations; and learning that thoughts are at least to some extent within the control of the thinker.

Similarly, clients' difficulties in accepting praise and accepting that they can do things well could become a target in the problem-solving process. This might initially be a problem identified by the worker, but come to be one which the client recognises as well. Strategies for addressing the problem might involve asking clients to identify things that they like about themselves. The use of products such as strengths cards, developed by an Australian Family Care agency to help clients identify their strengths, could be useful for this purpose (Scott and O'Neill 1996). Similarly, workers might help clients to identify their hopes for the future or to respond appropriately to the worker's positive comments.

In attempting to be optimistic, workers should be careful not to overdo it. Furstenberg and Rounds (1995), in their review of self-efficacy in social work, suggest that workers are more likely to be persuasive with clients if they are viewed as credible. The client must believe that the worker understands the nature of the client's world. In other words, optimism which recognises difficulties, rather than optimism which trivialises those difficulties, is more likely to be persuasive.

Finally, it is important that optimism is not confused with the notion of minimisation in work with involuntary clients. It is important that the worker believes in the capacity of the client to change. However, as emphasised in Chapter 4, it is also important that the worker in no way minimises the anti-social behaviour which has led the client to become a client.

# Humour

It was pointed out in Chapter 2 that the use of humour by workers may be related to client outcomes. Research dating back to the 1970s and 1980s (e.g. Alexander et al. 1978) has suggested that humour can be used to help clients to deal with and distance themselves from problems, defuse anger and 'provide an emotionally arousing dynamic for confronting, provocative insight giving and empathic helping procedures' (Siporin 1984:461).

Reference was also made in Chapter 2 to David Pollio (1995:378), who argues that 'positive outcomes of humour include breaking an impasse in the therapeutic process, reframing the context of the problem situation, freeing and empowering the client system and humanising the situation'. Daniel Eckstein (2003) suggests that humour can unblock barriers in the problem-solving process.

It certainly seems that humour can be used in emotional situations which the worker and/or the client find difficult to handle. There are instances when it is important for both worker and client to maintain sufficient composure to work through the problem-solving process, and some use of humour may enable them to do this. For example, a client discussing the recent death of a loved one might be encouraged to talk about some of the lighter moments of that person's life, leading to some laughter between worker and client.

Some guidelines on humour which might be useful to workers with involuntary clients are outlined below. These are developed from my reading of the literature and from comments made by professional workers in my workshops—although it should be emphasised that the research in this area is limited and the following guidelines are suggestions rather than developed principles of practice.

## Constructive humour

Humour which is likely to have positive outcomes includes humour which comes naturally to the situation and which is not contrived; humour which gives the client the sense that they are being treated as a person rather than merely as a client; humour which lightens an overly tense interview situation; humour which responds directly to the client's comments or which picks up on light or humorous comments by clients; and humour which acknowledges the client's feelings in a non-threatening way.

Some examples of humour which professional workers with involuntary clients have found constructive are illustrated in the following examples.

A female child protection worker has made many visits to a family and, while the worker has a good working relationship with the mother, the mother's partner has been very angry towards the worker, although on recent visits he has been more reasonable. When she visits, she is greeted by both parents at the door and the mother says: 'It is nice to see you.' The father mumbles something which also sounds like: 'It is nice to see you.' The worker says to the father: 'I am not hoping for "nice to see you" but we are progressing, aren't we?' All three laugh and the interview gets off to a good start.

The humour is used to acknowledge the clients' and the worker's feelings, to reinforce the progress in the relationship between the father and the worker, and to relieve the tension between them.

And another example—a woman who had been abused and placed in state care as a child now faces a similar situation with her oldest child being placed in foster care. In a long and tense interview with the foster care worker, the mother is talking about her contact with welfare agencies over the years. The worker comments: 'You must have seen about 50 different social workers over the past twenty years.' The client responds: 'It's more than that and not many of them have helped me.' The worker then says: 'You would think with all those social workers you would not have a problem in the world.'

Both laugh and it relieves some of the tenseness of the situation. Again, in this instance, the client's experience with so many social workers, and her cynicism about them, is acknowledged but it is done in a way which is not threatening to either worker or client.

## Destructive humour

Humour can be misused, however. David Pollio (1995) suggests that negative uses of humour include humour in which the client misinterprets the situation and humour which demeans the client or leaves the client confused. Some types of humour are certainly inappropriate—for example, humour which is used to avoid discussions about sensitive topics; humour which is in any way sarcastic or used to put down the client (or anyone else); humour which aims to show how clever the worker is; humour which gives clients the feeling that they are not being taken seriously; and the telling of jokes.

# Self-disclosure

Self-disclosure has been discussed a lot in the literature on counselling and psychotherapy. It is sometimes seen as a manifestation of worker genuineness or authenticity.

Robert Carkhuff (1969), in his work on effective counselling methods, suggests that self-disclosure is one of the key counselling skills. He developed a measure which can be used to rate the extent of self-disclosure by therapists or counsellors in interviews. Low levels of self-disclosure are characterised by the worker actively attempting to remain detached from the client and disclosing 'nothing of his own feelings or personality' (Carkhuff 1969:321). High levels of self-disclosure are characterised by the worker volunteering 'very intimate and often detailed material about his own personality'.

The extent to which self-disclosure is helpful in work with involuntary clients, and just how that self-disclosure should be offered, are uncertain. The difficulty of disentangling self-disclosure from other relationship factors and the lack of research on self-disclosure in work with involuntary clients contribute to this uncertainty.

Nonetheless, there are a number of guidelines which might be offered to assist workers in making decisions about self-disclosure. Self-disclosure which involves non-intimate details about a worker's life, such as whether the worker is married or has children, is generally appropriate, particularly in situations where clients are expected to disclose very personal material. This is consistent with research by Shulman (1991) and with the principles of pro-social modelling referred to in Chapter 4.

Self-disclosure may be particularly valuable if workers wish clients to disclose personal matters (Anderson and Mandell 1989). It seems that personal comments such as 'I found it very difficult when my children were young' or 'when I was unemployed' or 'after I separated from my partner' will encourage clients to disclose more personal material about themselves.

Self-disclosure or modelling which refers to difficulties the worker has experienced is likely to be more helpful than self-disclosure which refers to the worker's achievement (Derlega and Berg 1987). For example, a worker who talks about how she has been able to find work easily in the past is less likely to motivate a client than one who talks about how difficult it was to find work, and how she became quite depressed by the situation but was eventually successful.

Self-disclosure should not shift the focus of the interview from the client to the worker. Self-disclosures should be brief and used for the purpose of showing empathy for the client's situation. It hardly needs saying that the focus of interviews should be the client's problems rather than those of the worker.

Nor should self-disclosure be too intimate (Anderson and Mandell 1989). A comment that the worker found it very difficult to handle a broken relationship some years ago might be appropriate. However, a comment that the worker is in a state of depression following a recent marital breakdown is not likely to be appropriate.

Care should be used with clients who are likely to misinterpret self-disclosures. For example, self-disclosure may be inappropriate with some schizophrenic or heavily dependent clients.

Sandra Anderson and Deborah Mandell (1989) also suggest that self-disclosure should be mentioned as part of the role clarification: it should be pointed out that 'therapist self disclosure is an expected part of treatment'. In other words, the worker should explain that they may refer briefly to their own experiences to help them understand the way the client is feeling.

I mentioned in Chapter 2 that my child protection study sheds some light on this issue (Trotter 2004). Workers who used some self-disclosure tended to have clients with better outcomes, although the clients themselves did not see self-disclosure as particularly important.

The workers commented on situations in which they used self-disclosure. Fifty-seven per cent of the workers saw it as appropriate to talk about their interests and hobbies—for example, 'I am a keen tennis player or gardener'. Slightly fewer (51 per cent) felt that it was appropriate to comment on their own personal life experience in exploring problems and strategies—for example, a comment like 'I have found that admitting mistakes often helps me in my own relationships'. Fewer again (43 per cent) felt that it was appropriate to talk about their own situation in terms of whether they were married or had children and even fewer (40 per cent) felt that it was appropriate to comment on the demands of protective work or your feelings about the work—for example, 'I don't like having to come in here and tell you someone has made a report about you'.

To summarise: it does seem that some level of self-disclosure in work with involuntary clients is appropriate. While the extent and nature of this self-disclosure is largely dependent on the situation, the fear some workers have about self-disclosure appears to be inappropriate, particularly when this involves a reluctance to disclose even the most minor details while at the same time expecting detailed disclosures from clients.

# Client violence

Work with involuntary clients often involves working with clients who are both aggressive and violent. A number of studies have provided estimates of the extent to which workers with involuntary clients are the victims of physical assaults and threats of physical assaults and other intimidating behaviour by clients. Brian Littlechild (2002), in a review of the literature, points to one American study of social services workers which found that 3 per cent had been shot at. It also found that 25 per cent of correctional workers had been attacked with knives. Another American study suggests that 65 per cent of professional social workers had experienced client violence (Beaver 1999). On the other hand, Littlechild (2002) refers to a British study which found that less than 10 per cent of social workers and probation officers had experienced assaults.

An earlier Australian study by Tom Puckett and Helen Cleak (1994) found that 31 per cent of welfare workers had been physically assaulted during their careers, with many more having been abused verbally or threatened. The sample included social workers, welfare workers and youth workers working in a range of settings with predominantly involuntary clients. More than half the assaults took place at the client's residence and, perhaps surprisingly, more than half were in the presence of one or more of the worker's colleagues.

This issue needs to be placed in context. Most involuntary clients are not violent towards their workers. Puckett and Cleak (1994) cite studies, for example, which suggest that more than 90 per cent of clients do not pose any threat to workers. On the other hand, those clients who do pose a threat to workers may have a pervasive influence on worker stress levels and work satisfaction.

Judith Gibbs (2001), in an Australian study, found that child protection workers experiencing high levels of stress referred to physical and verbal attacks from clients along with issues such as job security and respect from managers and peers. Others have pointed to the impact that violence, threats of violence and intimidating client behaviour can have on the ability of workers to make accurate assessments and provide effective interventions. Janet Stanley and Chris Goddard (2002), for example, argue on the basis of their research in child protection that workers may underestimate the levels of violence within families because they feel intimidated and threatened.

A number of practical strategies have been suggested which might minimise the likelihood of becoming a victim of client violence (e.g. Rey 1996; Puckett and Cleak 1994; Littlechild 2002). Brian Littlechild (2002) argues that dealing with this issue is largely an organisational responsibility. He suggests that the stress and anxiety of workers relating to this issue may be reduced with good supervision and training which includes dealing with angry clients; a culture which does not blame the workers but allows workers to raise issues of concern without fear of being seen as weak or incompetent; debriefing for workers; and recording of incidents.

The following strategies may also help workers avoid violent situations:

- Interviews in client homes should be conducted at the front of the house so that the worker has access to the door in case they wish to make a quick exit. If workers feel unsafe, they should not enter the client's home.
- Workers should always inform someone from their office where they are going and if possible take a mobile phone.
- Interview rooms in offices should be set up so that the worker has ready access to the door and can leave the room quickly if necessary. A worker who has their desk away from the door, leaving the client between herself and the door, is vulnerable. An emergency alarm in interview rooms should be standard in work with involuntary clients. Interview rooms should not contain heavy objects. If possible, rooms should have two exits.
- If workers feel threatened, they should avoid confronting clients, and listen to what the client is saying. If the client has a sense that they are being listened to, it may reduce their frustration and aggression. The worker should then extricate themself from the situation as soon as possible.

Reference was made earlier to the increasing focus in some organisations on investigation and risk assessment, often at the expense of helping and therapeutic interventions. The potential for this focus to lead to resentment and anger on the part of clients is clear. The evidence cited throughout this book, however, suggests that, even in this environment, when workers have good skills their clients are not only likely to have good outcomes, but they are also likely to be satisfied with their workers. I do not want to minimise the potential impact of client violence and intimidation; however, its frequency is likely to be reduced if workers are able to balance their investigatory and helping roles, work through collaborative problem-solving processes and focus on their client's pro-social commmments and actions.

For more detailed strategies for preventing and dealing with client violence, see Newell (2003).

# Summary

The relationship is defined in this chapter as including empathy, optimism, humour and self-disclosure. Other texts include other factors in the relationship, such as the use of authority, confidentiality and genuineness. These factors are addressed in other sections of this book.

Empathy—or the ability to understand another's point of view— is a helpful skill in work with involuntary clients when it is accompanied by the other skills of problem-solving, pro-social modelling and role clarification. Optimistic workers seem to communicate this optimism to their clients, who in turn do better.

The worker's use of humour is an unresearched area in work with involuntary clients, but it does appear that appropriate use of humour may be related to positive outcomes. Similarly, little work has been done on the use of self-disclosure; however, there is some indication that it may contribute towards positive outcomes in work with involuntary clients. The chapter also considers worker safety.

# 7 WORKING WITH FAMILIES

Work with involuntary clients often involves working with  families. Probation officers may work with the parents and extended families of juvenile offenders, as well as the partners or extended family of adult offenders. Child protection workers work with the families of abused and neglected children. Mental health workers may work with family members, as do workers in domestic violence, school welfare, and youth work.

In work with involuntary clients, whole families may be clients— for example, in child protection, when a family might be placed under supervision by a court. Often, however, a single client is involuntary, and involvement with the client's family is on a more voluntary basis. For example, a probationer is an involuntary client, but the probationer's partner, or mother, is not an involuntary client.

The term 'family' is interpreted broadly in this book. Family members may, for example, include foster parents or same-sex partners. Family is defined as any two or more people who live in intimate relationships with one another.

# When is it appropriate to work with family groups?

It is possible to work with families as a family group or with family members individually. Working with a family group usually involves two or more family members working with a family worker through a range of problems or issues which are of concern to the family members.

Work on an individual basis with family members involves the worker seeing the different family members separately. Workers may, for example, work with the family members of a mental health client independently from that client. Workers might spend time educating family members about the nature of the mental illness and the role they might play in supporting the client. This should, of course, occur with the client's knowledge and as part of a problem-solving process; nonetheless, the client may not be directly involved in the work with other family members.

Work with the family group is likely to be more appropriate in some circumstances than others. It is unlikely to be appropriate when a client's problems are clearly individual problems—in situations where there is no apparent link between the client's problems and other family members. Nor is family work likely to be appropriate if the client does not live with or interact closely with other family members.

Work with family groups is generally not appropriate with the perpetrator and victim of sexual or physical assault. This is not to say that there are never occasions when work with a perpetrator and a victim is appropriate. For example, a perpetrator who understands the damage that his actions have caused might apologise to the victim for his actions. This could take place in a family counselling session as part of a plan to help a victim deal with issues of guilt. However, generally speaking, family work which makes use of a mediation style, as described later in this chapter, is unlikely to be appropriate in situations where one family member is clearly a victim of sexual or physical assault and another a perpetrator of that assault.

Where it is apparent to the worker that there is a severe power imbalance in the family, family groupwork is unlikely to be appropriate. For example, a father might be very dominant in the family situation and other family members intimidated by him and afraid to express their ideas in his presence. Individual work might be more appropriate in this instance. The worker might work on these issues with the father with a view to involving the family group at a later stage. In the short term, however, family work as it is described in this chapter assumes that family members feel free to express their views without fear of retribution.

In situations where the worker has a value clash with certain family members, family groupwork is also likely to be inappropriate. For example, a worker might feel unable to work with parents who will not allow their twenty-year-old daughter to go out with men alone. In this instance, working individually with the parents and the daughter might be more appropriate.

On the other hand, it was argued in Chapter 2 that there are many instances in work with involuntary clients when it may be more appropriate to work with a family group rather than with individuals. The positive outcomes achieved in some family counselling programs certainly suggest this (e.g. Sexton and Alexander 2002).

Working with a family group is likely to be appropriate in situations where issues raised by the client are related to family interaction patterns; where family interaction patterns appear to relate to the reason the client is a client (e.g. a young person who offends after being told to leave home); and where increased levels of understanding of each other's point of view is likely to help family interaction.

In situations where individual work is being carried out, it may become apparent that family work is the most appropriate method of dealing with a particular problem. For example, if in working through the problem-solving process a probationer identifies problems in his relationship with his partner, a task might be set to work through issues in one or more joint sessions with that partner.

# Collaborative family counselling

There are many family therapy, family counselling and family mediation models which have been used in work with both voluntary and involuntary clients. Irene and Herbert Goldenberg (2004), for example, refer to more than twenty different family therapies. Some examples, just to mention a few, include structural, experiential, trans-generational, systems, cognitive behavioural, solution-focused and narrative therapies.

It is not within the scope of this book to examine the range of family therapy models in any detail. The aim is rather to introduce a model of family work which is a development of the effective practice principles outlined earlier in the book.

Work with the family group is often the most appropriate way of working with involuntary clients. Workers may, of course, refer families for specialist family counselling; however, in many instances it may be more appropriate for the worker to do the work with the family herself. Sometimes family counselling may be unavailable. On other occasions the family may be more comfortable working with someone they already know and trust. As discussed earlier, there are advantages in minimising the number of workers in clients' lives.

This chapter outlines a model for working with families which I am referring to as *collaborative family counselling*. The model includes role clarification, pro-social modelling and reinforcement, problem-solving and the client–worker relationship. In other words, it involves the application of the effective practice skills outlined in this book to work with families. While the model is distinctive in combining these four practice components, it is acknowledged that the problem-solving aspects of the model are similar to earlier family problem-solving models developed by Epstein and Bishop (1981), Forgatch and Patterson (1989) and Reid (1985, 1992).

I have chosen to present this particular family work model for several reasons. It is consistent with the general principles of effective practice, and as such the model builds on the skills which effective workers with involuntary clients already possess. For this reason, it can be learned relatively quickly by workers with some professional training and/or experience. My research with both social work students and professional welfare workers (Trotter 1997b, 2000; Trotter, Cox and Crawford 2002) found that, even though they had minimal experience in family counselling, they were able to successfully carry out a series of family counselling sessions after about sixteen hours of training.

As pointed out in Chapter 2, family work using similar types of intervention models has been used and tested in work with a range of involuntary clients in such settings as child protection, juvenile justice, mental health and youth work (Reid 1985, 1992; Perkins-Dock 2001; Sexton and Alexander 2002). As I mentioned in Chapter 2, 100 per cent of the clients in my research, many of whom were involuntary, indicated that they benefited from collaborative family counselling (Trotter 2000).

# A home-based model

Family counselling sessions may be held in the worker's office or in the family's home. Home-based sessions have advantages, and the students and professionals who participated in my research studies have undertaken most of the sessions in the family home. Certainly, family members are more likely to participate. Our experience in the Australian studies was that often one or two family members would miss sessions when they were office-based; however, this was rare when they were home-based. Family members are often more comfortable in their own homes and home-based work provides the counsellor with an opportunity to see how the family interacts in the home environment. It also often helps to reduce the power differential, and hence increase the sense of partnership.

On the other hand, there may be issues of worker safety which must take precedence over any therapeutic advantages. It also may be difficult to maintain control of the sessions in the home environment. Telephone calls, visitors or trips to the kitchen or the bedroom by different family members can be disruptive and interrupt the flow of the sessions. These issues present a challenge for the worker; however, if they can be overcome then the family home is the preferable venue for the counselling.

# The collaborative family counselling process

The model outlined below involves using the practice skills developed in this book. It involves working through each of the steps in the problem-solving model presented in Chapter 5: problem survey; problem ranking; problem exploration; setting goals; developing a contract; strategies and tasks; and review.

Collaborative family work can be undertaken with two or more family members. Ideally, all family members caught in the family dynamics should be involved; however, the process can still work well if only some members of the family choose to participate. Children should be able to participate in the process if they are old enough to follow the discussion, usually from around ten years of age.

## Preparation for family work

It is important that family members are prepared for the family sessions before the first session. This preparation begins the role-clarification process. The aim is to help individual family members understand the purpose of the work, what will be expected of them in the process and how long it will take. It may involve clarifying misapprehensions about the family counselling process or discussing previous experiences the family members may have had with family counselling. An individual discussion with each family member before work with the family group begins is likely to get the family group sessions off to a good start.

This may be particularly important if the client family does not share a similar cultural background to the worker. If the clients ascribe particular roles to different family members—for example, that the father is head of the family—or if the family members are unaccustomed to discussing problems on an equal basis, this should be addressed before the counselling session begins.

## Role clarification

A number of issues should be addressed in helping the family members understand the role of the worker and of the family members in the family counselling process.

It should be explained at the outset that the worker aims to take a neutral stance—that no one person's point of view will be supported over another's, and that the aim is to reach agreement between family members. On the other hand, the worker may have a specific mandate to reduce the likelihood of a young person reoffending or to ensure that child abuse does not reoccur. In these instances, the worker would make this clear to the family members but explain that she still wishes to work on a collaborative model to address issues which may have in some way contributed to the offending or child abuse.

The worker should discuss the number of sessions which will be undertaken and who should attend the sessions. The worker may, for example, seek a commitment from family members to attend a certain number of sessions if she feels this is necessary to make progress on the issues facing the family.

The worker should discuss the issue of confidentiality. Will what goes on in the sessions be kept within the sessions? What is the responsibility of the worker if further offending or child abuse is mentioned in the sessions? What if one of the family members wishes to talk to the worker between sessions—is this OK and would these discussions be confidential?

The worker should ask each of the family members what they hope to get out of the sessions. The clients should be asked what they expect from the counselling. Have the family members experienced family counselling before? What was this like? Do any family members have preconceptions about what family counselling should be?

The worker should also introduce the family problem-solving model to the client family and explain how it works, particularly its focus on helping the family to solve problems themselves. Workers in my research projects have taken blown-up copies of the problem-solving steps to family homes so that family members can follow the steps of the model as the sessions progress. If the interview is conducted in the family home, a piece of paper outlining the steps might be given to family members (see Appendix for an outline of the problem-solving steps).

The worker should help the family members to reach agreement regarding ground rules for the sessions. Ground rules might include that each family member is to allow other family members to speak uninterrupted; that they are free to ask for clarification of points but otherwise they should listen to the speaker until he has finished; that participants are expected not to shout or be abusive; or that family members may leave if they feel uncomfortable. Setting ground rules such as these at the outset is likely to facilitate a less volatile counselling process. It also provides an opportunity for the family to learn and practise the process of reaching agreement through discussion. The process of developing ground rules can represent the beginning of improved communication between family members.

## Problem survey

The purpose of the family problem survey, like the problem survey with individual clients, is to identify issues which are of concern to family members. The worker asks family members to describe in turn issues which are of concern to them, or things about family relationships which they would like to change. As each person identifies issues or problems, the worker writes these down in the person's own words, either in file notes or on a white board. It is important that the family members are able to see the list as it is written.

It might be appropriate to ask the less powerful, or least forceful, family members to speak first to encourage an equal involvement in the process. It might also be appropriate to specify that each family member has a specific time to talk about their issues—say, up to five minutes—to ensure that particular family members do not dominate.

The worker should encourage family members to express problems in non-blaming terms. For example, the worker might reframe problems for the client. A twelve-year-old girl might say that her biggest problem is her fourteen-year-old sister—'She goes out whenever she likes and I have to stay home'. Following some further discussion, the girl might be encouraged to reframe her problem as: 'It upsets me that my mother has different rules about what my sister is allowed to do and what I am allowed to do. I feel like she thinks she cannot trust me.'

Care must of course be exercised to ensure that reframing does not involve the worker restating the problem as the worker sees it. As emphasised throughout this book, it is vital that the problem to be worked on is in fact the client's problem.

The worker should prompt family members to identify problems which are likely to be related to the client's status as an involuntary client. For example, the worker might ask a young person who has been truanting from school to talk about whether school presents a problem for her. Or the worker could ask a young person who has been running away from home to identify specific things he does not like about home.

At the problem survey stage, while some clarification of issues is appropriate, the worker should encourage each client to be brief. Further discussion of the issues can take place later. In the early stages, it is important that other family members don't have to wait too long to get a turn.

Once each person has spoken, and the worker has a written list of all the issues, the worker should try to identify the common concerns. If none of the problems expressed by the different family members seems to be the same the worker should try to reframe or redefine the problems as common problems. For example, it may be that a mother is concerned about her daughter's truancy. The daughter may not be worried about her truancy, but might be distressed about her mother's angry outbursts about her truancy. There is therefore a common concern about school. The common problem is disagreement about school attendance, so the problem could be defined in this way.

To take another example, a young person may be concerned that his mother is hardly ever home. In this instance, the worker might ask other family members whether this is a problem for them. The worker might ask the mother if she is concerned about the amount of time she is able to spend with her son. It might in this way be possible to define the problem as a common family problem.

Family members may also have problems which are of concern only to themselves, and these can better be dealt with at the individual level. For example, a mother might be unhappy in a relationship with one of her friends, but her son may feel this is of no concern to him.

Thus, at the completion of the problem survey, the worker should have a list of problems for each family member. As far as possible, these problems should be defined as common problems; however, it may be that some individual problems will remain.

## Problem ranking

The aim is then to make a decision about which problem or problems to work on. The worker should keep in mind the guidelines for problem ranking referred to in Chapter 5. The problems to be worked on should be the family's own problems; they should as far as possible be problems that are amenable to change, and for which resources are available; they should be related to the worker's own goals for the family; and they should relate to practical rather than intra-psychic issues.

It is vital to work with the family's problems as the family members define them. The worker might suggest which problems are most appropriate to begin with; however, the family must agree that the problems to be worked on are important. If family members have different problems, it may be necessary to work simultaneously on one problem for each family member.

Solvable problems should be addressed first. It might be best, for example, to start with a problem about pocket money rather than a problem relating to a parent who is not involved in the counselling and has no interest in the family.

It is also better to deal with problems for which there are resources available to help. For example, if the family has a problem with inadequate housing, then it is much easier to deal with this if there is a possibility of getting better housing.

If one family member is subject to some formal mandate or authority, it may be appropriate to start with the formal requirements. For example, if a child is to be expelled from school unless certain things occur, or if a young person is required to undertake certain actions as part of a court order, these problems should take precedence.

The problem-solving model focuses on practical issues or problems. As far as possible, the focus should be issues such as housing, employment or drug use, rather than intra-psychic issues such as self-esteem, anxiety or depression.

Finally, if the family or any family members are facing some immediate crisis, this might need to be dealt with first. For example, if the family is homeless, this would probably have to take immediate priority.

Taking these factors into account, the worker should encourage the family to agree on the most appropriate family problem to begin work on. If it is not possible to reach agreement on which problem to work on, it may be appropriate to work on more than one problem. The family members should feel that at least one of the problems to be worked on is relevant to them.

## Problem exploration

Some problem exploration will have taken place during the problem survey. Nonetheless, it is appropriate to gather some more information about the problem before moving on to goals and solutions. It is important that the family members and the worker have a thorough picture of the problem before strategies for solving it are developed.

As suggested in Chapter 5, in relation to individual problem-solving, the family members should be asked about the history of the problem.

When does it occur? How did it begin? What has the family done to address the problem previously? Have these things helped or hindered? What is sustaining the problem? Are there occasions when the problem is not present? What is different on these occasions? Can these occasions be increased?

## Goal-setting

The next step involves setting goals—clear and specific goals which are agreed to by the worker and the clients and are directly related to the problem(s). The goals answer the question: what does the family want to happen? Examples of goals might include:

- For Tony to move out of home within two weeks.
- For Zac and her spouse Mike to make a decision about whether or not Zac should seek inpatient treatment in relation to alcohol addiction.
- For all instances of domestic violence to cease immediately.

The goals should be as specific as possible so that it is clear to the worker and the client at a later date whether or not the goal has been achieved.

## Contract

When the family members have reached agreement about what they wish to achieve, a written contract should be developed summarising the problems to be worked on, the goals to be achieved, and any ground rules or expectations the worker or the client might have in relation to the family problem-solving process. See the following box for an example of a family problem-solving contract relating to a fifteen-year-old girl, Amy, who has been placed on probation for stealing which occurred when she ran away with her nineteen-year-old boyfriend.

# Family problem-solving contract

## Problems

1. Amy and Mrs Larkin (Amy's mother) are worried about Amy being unhappy at home and about her wanting to run away from home again.
2. Amy and Mrs Larkin argue constantly, and rarely if ever talk in a civil manner to each other.
3. Amy and Mrs Larkin are unable to agree on whether or how often Amy sees her boyfriend.
4. Amy and Mrs Larkin are concerned about school. Amy is concerned because she feels school offers her nothing but is unsure what else to do and Mrs L. is worried that Amy will miss out on opportunities if she does not stay at school.

## Goals

1. For Amy to live at home with her mother and brother on an ongoing basis.
2. For Amy and Mrs L. to report to the worker that they talk to each other in a friendly way and listen to each other for at least five minutes on at least two occasions each week. The aim is for this goal to be achieved by Week 3.
3. For Amy and Mrs L. to reach agreement on whether Amy should continue to see her boyfriend and, if so, how often and where she should see him. This goal to be achieved by Week 7.
4. For Amy and Mrs L. to make a decision about whether Amy should stay at school or look for some other way of occupying her time. This goal is to be achieved by Week 8.

## Ground rules for the family counselling sessions

1. Amy and Mrs L. to attend each session or explain to the counsellor and each other why they are unable to attend. Initially ten sessions will be held.
2. Amy, Mrs L. and the counsellor to listen to each other in counselling sessions and not to interrupt each other except to clarify what is being said.

3. Amy or Mrs L. are free to ask for individual sessions with the counsellors if they wish. These sessions will be confidential.
4. No information to be given to any other people about what goes on in the sessions without the permission of Amy and Mrs L.

## Strategies/tasks

Strategies or tasks should then be developed by the worker and family members to address the goals. As outlined in Chapter 5, strategies or tasks might be carried out inside or outside the counselling sessions.

The following are examples of tasks which might be carried out during the sessions. These tasks relate particularly to goals relating to improved communication or reducing arguments within the family.

- Family members could be asked to listen to each other for a specific period of time (e.g. three minutes) and then be asked to paraphrase what has been said. The aim of this task is to teach listening skills, which should in turn help to improve communication and reduce the number of arguments.
- Another task relating to communication might involve the use of role play. The worker might ask a mother and her daughter to role play a situation in which arguments commonly occur—for example, a discussion about a boyfriend. Then, rather than arguing as they normally do, they could be asked to focus on listening to the other person and paraphrasing what has been said.
- Family members can be asked to reverse roles so that the mother takes the daughter's role and vice versa. This could help them to understand what the situation is like from the other person's point of view.
- Another task, which was used often by workers in my research projects, involves teaching clients to give each other positive feedback. Family members might be asked to brainstorm all of the things they like, appreciate or admire about each other, and these

might be listed on a piece of paper or on the board by the worker. In families where a negative pattern of interaction has developed, positive comments may be rare. Articulating positives can have a powerful impact.

- Another task, which might be carried out in the interview setting, involves brainstorming solutions. For example, the family members might agree on a goal which involves a young person continuing to live in the family home for at least the next three months. Family members, including the young person, could then be asked to think of anything which might encourage the young person to remain at home. These ideas could then be listed on a board or piece of paper and worked through to see if they could be developed into specific tasks. Tasks developed in this manner might then be carried out during sessions—for example, talking about what family members like about each other.

- Tasks carried out at home between sessions could involve, for example, engaging in mutually enjoyable activities, or spending a specified time together. Other home tasks might involve extended family members. For example, the goal may emerge in discussions between family members for a young person to have more contact with a suitable adult role model. It may be that increased contact can be facilitated with an uncle or another relative. It might, in this instance, even be appropriate to involve the uncle in the family counselling sessions so he can help to develop the task.

Sometimes simple tasks can be very powerful. One particularly interesting example is drawn from the practice of a worker in one of my research projects. A twelve-year-old boy, Danuka, was placed on probation following a number of serious offences. He committed these offences after running away from home. He ran away from home often, sometimes staying away for days at a time. His parents did not know where he stayed when he was away from home. A brainstorming task was used with this family, in which the mother, father and Danuka all suggested things which might stop Danuka from running away in the future. Danuka said that he would enjoy home more if someone would play chess with him.

A task was subsequently set for Danuka and his father to play chess once per week (subsequently increased to twice per week). The chess playing continued during and after the family's involvement in family counselling, and it seemed to be highly influential in persuading Danuka to stay at home. The task seemed to allow for the attention Danuka wanted from his father, and their relationship improved dramatically. The offending also stopped.

This seems like such a simple solution to a very complex problem. Its success seemed to lie in the fact that it was a task suggested and designed by Danuka, and it addressed what was perhaps Danuka's core problem—his relationship with his father. The problem was addressed in a positive way, the task was easily carried out, and it implied no blame or fault on the part of either Danuka or his father.

## Ongoing review

The final step in the collaborative family counselling process relates to ongoing monitoring or review. This recognises that it is necessary to continually revise the stages you are at in the problem-solving process. While the steps are straightforward, families do not tend to organise their problems with problem-solving processes in mind. The worker should aim to use the problem-solving structure to make sense of the counselling process; however, the structure should be used flexibly.

# Pro-social modelling

It is important during the family counselling process that the worker models pro-social behaviour, reinforces pro-social behaviour in family members and challenges pro-criminal or anti-social comments by family members—in the same way as in work with individual clients. While the worker may be neutral in terms of not favouring particular family members, and in trying to develop collaboration, she should—as in work with individuals—encourage pro-social comments and actions on the part of family members. This includes encouraging and rewarding the ongoing involvement of family members in the family problem-solving process. Family members should be encouraged and rewarded for attending sessions, identifying problems, following through on tasks and generally participating in the process.

The focus on positives provided by pro-social modelling and reinforcement is important because it provides a balance to the discussions about problems. It is also important that, in challenging pro-criminal and anti-social comments, the worker is cautious not to be seen to be taking sides or being critical of individual family members. While it is important that pro-criminal and anti-social comments are not ignored, it is equally important that challenges follow the principles of confrontation referred to in Chapter 4.

# The worker–client relationship

In undertaking collaborative family work, the worker should make use of the relationship skills referred to in Chapter 6. The worker should listen to and try to understand the point of view of each family member. They should be optimistic about the potential of the family to change and about the potential of collaborative family work to make a difference. They should not be afraid to use some humour and some self-disclosure to help family members to feel relaxed and comfortable.

## *Collaborative family counselling—a case example*

Outlined below is an example of the collaborative family work process. In the example, names and identifying details have been changed; however, the details of the intervention are as they were described to me by one of the workers involved in my family counselling research project referred to earlier (Trotter 1997b, 2000, 2002). I have presented the case study as it occurred, even though it contains some practices which may not be entirely consistent with the collaborative family work model—for example, the task set by the worker for the mother and daughter to hug each other.

Laura ran away from home at the age of fourteen following a series of arguments with her mother and sister. She stayed with friends for a few days and then approached a youth counselling service for financial assistance. She was subsequently placed in three successive supported accommodation placements over a period of a year; however, each placement broke down. The third and final placement broke down due to Laura's extreme introversion, her inappropriate sexual behaviour, her chronic bed-wetting and her violence toward other residents.

She was referred for a psychiatric assessment because of concerns about her bed-wetting and her other problems. The psychiatrist, however, indicated that she had no diagnosable psychiatric illness.

Laura was almost sixteen by this stage, and she was told that the agency could no longer provide accommodation for her. Laura's mother, Anne, had expressed a willingness to have Laura return home. It was put to Laura that she would have to return to live with her mother unless she could work out some other arrangement.

Laura was clear that she did not wish to return home and refused to discuss with workers where she was going to live. At this stage, the worker put a proposal to Laura, asking her to attend six family counselling sessions with her mother. It was put to her that if she completed the counselling sessions and still did not wish to return home, the worker would do her best to assist her to find alternative accommodation. Laura agreed on this basis. Laura's mother was also agreeable to the arrangement.

Laura was not, therefore, entirely an involuntary client. At nearly sixteen she could have gone her own way and sorted out her own accommodation, and there would have been no legal sanction. On the other hand, she had many personal and interpersonal problems, and her placement options were very limited. While she could be defined as partially voluntary, she might be placed more toward the involuntary end of the involuntary–voluntary client continuum because of her resistance to being involved in the family counselling process.

Laura and her mother subsequently attended five collaborative family counselling sessions with a youth worker at the agency. The mother attended the sixth session alone.

The first meeting was the first time Laura and her mother had met since Laura left home. They had had some phone contact over the past year, but had not seen each other during this period. The initial meeting was tense, with Laura refusing to look at or speak to her mother. The worker began with a discussion about roles and the nature of the family counselling process. Laura and her mother were then asked to identify issues which were concerning them.

Anne talked about the problems leading up to Laura leaving home. She said that she felt that Laura leaving home and refusing to return was an over-reaction to the situation. She said that her leaving was precipitated by an argument between Laura and her sister, by Laura's problems at school and by Laura's distress about her mother talking to teachers about her. She said Laura was also upset about her mother not allowing her to change schools.

Laura then talked about her problems. She said that she left home only after her mother dragged her outside and threatened to kill her. Laura said she felt and still feels unwanted, and that her mother and sister do not care about her opinions. She was unhappy about being told to stay home by her mother as punishment, her mother not talking to her and not liking her friends, and her mother talking to schoolteachers behind her back.

Following some discussion, Laura stated that she did not wish to discuss going home. Laura and her mother agreed that there was a problem of communication between them. Some tasks were then suggested by the worker, Laura and Anne in relation to a short-term goal of improved communication.

The tasks included:

- Having a telephone discussion before the next session.
- Anne to leave the decision about coming home to Laura and not to ask her to come home.
- Laura not to say that she would never come home.

These tasks were agreed to. At the next session, the tasks were reviewed. Anne had rung and they had had a conversation without argument. Laura described it as a 'normal' conversation. No mention was made of Laura coming home. Laura also rang home and spoke to her sister. (She rang for her mother but Anne was not home.)

This was the first contact between Laura and her family (outside the counselling session) for many months, and both Laura and her mother were congratulated by the worker on the successful completion of the task.

The worker then returned to the problem survey and asked Laura and Anne to identify the problems again. They agreed that blaming was a problem and forgiving (or an inability to do so) was a problem. These were problems for both Anne and Laura. There was also a problem with Anne expecting Laura to come home. When Anne mentioned this, Laura would get angry and insist that it was not her (Anne's) decision.

Goals were discussed, and Laura said that her goal in relation to the problem of forgiving was to not feel angry toward her mother any more. Laura's goal in relation to communication was to talk with her mother more. A goal for both Laura and Anne was not to talk about Laura coming home at this stage. Laura and Anne were able to agree to goals relating to improved communication and forgiving each other.

A number of tasks were suggested by Laura and her mother in relation to the goals of forgiving each other. Laura suggested that her mother apologise for threatening to kill her. Anne was not agreeable to this task. Anne then suggested that Laura go to her family home for afternoon tea next week. All agreed to this. With Anne's encouragement, Laura said she would go home after school on Tuesday, Wednesday and Thursday. This was agreed to.

At the next meeting, Laura had not carried out the tasks which had been set. She said she did not have time. Laura then said that she hated her mother and her mother hated her. Laura began to talk about how prior to her leaving home more than one year ago, her mother had forced her to go on access visits with her father and how her father had hit her during those visits.

Laura became very emotional and started to cry. She spoke directly to her mother about her feelings. She said that she had explained to her mother at the time that she was scared of her father and she was still forced to go. She felt betrayed by her mother.

The worker allowed this exchange to go for a long period because Anne was listening and Laura was expressing her feelings. As the conversation continued, Anne also started to cry. She said that she had not realised how serious the violence by Laura's father was and how much the visits upset Laura.

This outpouring of emotion and feeling from Laura could be defined as a spontaneously developed task for Laura to talk about her feelings. For the first time, her mother listened to and understood Laura's feelings about the abuse perpetrated by her father. It was a powerful moment in the counselling sessions because it was the first time Laura and Anne had seriously discussed this issue.

Toward the end of the session, the worker suggested that Laura and Anne hug each other. Laura at first responded 'no way'; however, it was put to her that this could be viewed as a task which might help both forgiveness and communication. They hugged in a somewhat strained manner. The worker felt that this session task allowed the session to finish on a very positive note.

Immediately after the meeting, the worker spoke to Laura and indicated that her time was running out at the supported accommodation placement and that she would have to leave. The worker hoped at this stage that Laura would agree to go home. Laura agreed to 'give it a try'. This marked a dramatic change in Laura, who before the family problem-solving sessions had barely spoken to her mother in twelve months. The change seemed to relate directly to the movement toward 'forgiving' her mother following the discussions about the abuse by her father.

The next family session took place three days after Laura returned to live with her family. Laura and Anne were both quite happy with the way things had gone for the three days; however, they agreed to keep working on the problems which had been defined in the previous sessions: those of forgiving each other and improved communication with each other.

A task, proposed by the worker, was to be carried out between sessions. The task involved talking to each other for at least ten minutes each day and not raising the past in any blaming way.

The next session occurred one week later. Laura had had an argument with her sister during the week and had hit her. The task of talking had not occurred, although there had been no raising of past matters by Laura or her mother.

Laura raised other problems. The worker then returned to the problem survey and added these problems to the issues of forgiveness and communication. Laura said her mother yelled at her more than her sister. She also added that she (Laura) was not interested in any long-term relationship with her mother.

Anne was concerned about Laura's swearing and the fact that she had hit her sister.

Two goals were then defined: Laura wanted her mother to yell at her less and Anne wanted Laura to stop swearing.

Tasks were discussed to address these problems. *Quid pro quo* or contingency tasks were agreed to. Laura agreed to stop swearing or at least using the 'f' and 'c' words which upset her mother. Anne said she would not yell at Laura.

There was further discussion about the problem of the abuse by the father. Anne talked about how she had been required to facilitate access between Laura and her father, and how she had felt powerless to prevent it. Further, she said that she had not realised how serious the violence was. Laura and Anne were again in tears in this discussion. The worker, in encouraging the forgiveness, pointed out to Anne and Laura that Laura's anger should more appropriately be directed towards her father, who was the perpetrator of the abuse.

Both Laura and Anne agreed that they needed to forgive each other. The discussion about this issue and Anne's explanation of her thoughts at the time constituted a session task toward the goal of forgiveness.

The session finished with Anne and Laura agreeing to try to carry out the tasks relating to swearing and yelling between this and the next session.

A final visit was scheduled; however, only Anne attended the last visit. Anne passed on a message from Laura that she was home now and so she did not have to come. Anne felt that the family counselling process had been very helpful, primarily because it had helped Laura to decide to return home to live and had helped her (Anne) to better understand her daughter.

A follow-up contact with Anne more than one year later indicated that Laura had remained at home with her mother and sister for one year. While they still had problems, they were clearly a family unit. Laura continued at school and satisfactorily completed Year 10. She subsequently moved out of home to live with a friend, but was still keeping in contact with her mother and attending school. She continued to have no contact with her father, her clearly expressed wish. While Laura had not wished to raise the issue of bed-wetting in the family counselling sessions, this too had subsided and was no longer a chronic problem.

This case study illustrates how collaborative family work can be used to facilitate communication between family members, even when there are long-standing communication problems. It also illustrates the flexible way in which the model is used, with movement between the problem survey, goals and tasks within sessions and between sessions. It can be described as a successful intervention—it is likely that Laura would not have returned to live with her mother without this family counselling experience.

# Summary

There are many different approaches to working with families. One of those approaches, collaborative family work, is discussed in this chapter. This model has been chosen because it is an application of the effective practice principles discussed in the earlier chapters of this book—role clarification, pro-social modelling, problem-solving and the client–worker relationship. The model is consistent with the research about what works, and it has some research support as an effective method for working with involuntary clients.

# 8 EVALUATION

Workers dealing with involuntary clients derive their knowledge for practice from a variety of sources. These include theories, models, research findings, values and beliefs, experience and organisational expectations. I have argued in favour of an evidence-based approach to direct practice—in other words, an approach which makes use of research findings as a primary source of knowledge for practice. I have suggested that, in using an evidence-based approach, workers should be clear about the purpose of their intervention and the values they wish to encourage.

I have also argued that the use of the practice model presented in this book will increase the likelihood that client and worker goals will be achieved. Evidence-based practice cannot, however, guarantee that work in any given instance will be successful. It may be that a worker will spend time exploring the concept of role with their client, will model and reinforce pro-social expressions, and will work through a client-oriented problem-solving process in a manner which is consistent with what the research says works. Yet, despite this, the client may not improve. They might abuse their children again, retreat to the use of drugs, be readmitted to hospital or end up in gaol.

Evidence-based practice has its limitations. Sometimes personal or environmental influences on the client are so strong that the client deteriorates despite the good work of the worker. In other instances, the generalised messages from research are insufficient to guide specific interventions. In these instances, workers must make individual judgments about how they work with their clients. For example, the research knowledge about when it is appropriate to use self-disclosure or humour is limited. Getting the balance right between the use of empathy, a focus on pro-social actions and expressions, and challenging rationalisations can also be difficult. Direct practice inevitably requires difficult individual judgments.

In many instances, it will not be clear whether a client has made progress in relation to the general presenting problem such as drug use, child abuse or offending. In other instances, workers may have this information, but it may relate only to the period of contact rather than the longer term.

How can a worker know whether a client is improving as a result of the intervention which is being offered?

This chapter outlines two approaches which can assist workers to evaluate their own work, both of which provide some ongoing information to workers about client progress and about their own intervention style. The first approach, *single case study evaluation*, aims to help workers know whether their clients have progressed during their intervention. The second, which I refer to as *case analysis*, involves workers examining how they have worked with their clients and how they might have done things differently.

It is not within the scope of this book to provide a comprehensive examination of evaluation procedures, and these approaches are dealt with only briefly. More has been written elsewhere about single case study research (e.g. Rubin and Babbie 2005) and about case analysis (e.g. Harkness and Hensley 1991; Fook 1996). The aim here is simply to present a few practical strategies which might assist workers to evaluate some of their day-to-day work.

# Single case study evaluation

Single case study evaluation involves systematically evaluating the progress of the client against specific objectives through the course of the intervention. It generally involves the client commenting on their progress.

Client evaluations are, of course, only one measure of effectiveness, and perhaps less persuasive than hard data measures like reoffending, more hospital admissions or further notifications of abuse. Nonetheless, client perspectives have value in their own right. Additionally, some research suggests that positive client evaluations tend to correlate with positive hard data evaluations (LaSala 1997; Trotter 1996a, 2004). In other words, clients seem to know if they are being helped.

Single case study evaluations vary in their complexity. At the lowest level, single case study evaluation might involve the worker simply asking the client to rate the extent to which goals and objectives have been achieved. This might involve a review which is little different from the review stage of the problem-solving process. In fact, the faithful application of the problem-solving process should provide the worker with considerable information about the progress of the client. The worker and the client should discuss, both during and at the conclusion of the intervention, the progress the client has made in relation to the goals which have been set.

The worker and the client might also discuss the feelings and views of the client about the direct practice process and the extent to which it has been helpful. The worker might ask the client what other things could have been done or said which might have helped the client.

It has been my experience that workers with involuntary clients for the most part finish their contact with their clients without taking advantage of the opportunity to talk to them about their experiences of the direct practice process. How did you find this contact? Did it help you? Were there things I might have done differently? The answers to these questions can help workers to develop a more effective style of working. In my view, it is the very least one might expect from professional workers. Organisations dealing with involuntary clients would do well to incorporate such practices into their standard documents, practice manuals and report forms.

At the next level of single case study methods, workers might use ongoing evaluation procedures with their clients in relation to general progress and in relation to specific problems. The box below presents client monitoring forms which were used in my collaborative family work research (Trotter 1997b, 2000, 2002).

Workers in the family problem-solving research project completed these forms with families at each session. The accumulating forms provided an ongoing assessment by the family of progress in relation to the specific problems which were being addressed, and in relation to general family relationships.

The information from such forms can then be presented on a graph to provide a more visual demonstration of the client's progress in relation to the particular issues which have been addressed. An example is shown in Figure 8.1. (Note that this type of evaluation can of course be used in direct practice with individuals as well as families.)

## *Client monitoring forms*

### *Rating scale for problems*

To be completed by the workers or family members at each session. One rating scale should be completed by each family member.

Circle a number on the scale 1 to 5 that corresponds to how you feel about the problem.

| 1 | 2 | 3 | 4 | 5 |
|---|---|---|---|---|

1. The problem is very serious and makes it very difficult to cope with everyday life.
2. The problem is very serious but you are able to cope with most everyday tasks.
3. The problem is serious but does not interfere with your everyday life.
4. The problem is not that serious and you are able to cope with it reasonably well.
5. There is no real problem.

## *General family functioning rating scale*

To be completed by the worker or family member at each session for each family member.

Circle a number on the scale 1 to 5 that corresponds with how you feel about the family.

| 1 | 2 | 3 | 4 | 5 |

Family relationships in our family at the present time are:

1. Poor, that is continual arguing, people rarely speak to each other, there is virtually no communication other than to dispute things.
2. Unsatisfactory, that is there is some positive communication between at least some family members, however overall family relationships are problematic and/or unsatisfying.
3. Satisfactory, that is family members communicate on some issues and there is some satisfaction in family life although things could be a lot better.
4. Very satisfactory, that is basically things are OK within the family and family members generally communicate without too much problem. Things still could be better however.
5. Good, that is family life is not characterised by arguments or poor communication and family members find it generally satisfying.

**Figure 8.1   Client assessment of family functioning over a 10 week intervention using the general family functioning rating scale**

| Week | 1 | 2 | 3 | 4 | 5 | 6 | 7 | 8 | 9 | 10 |
|---|---|---|---|---|---|---|---|---|---|---|
| 5 | | | | | | | | X | | X |
| 4 | | | | | | | X | | X | |
| 3 | | | | | | X | | | | |
| 2 | | | X | X | X | | | | | |
| 1 | X | X | | | | | | | | |

This type of single case study evaluation can, of course, also be used with hard data measures such as school attendance.

This level of single case study evaluation is relatively easy to administer, takes only a few minutes, in no way compromises the direct practice process and provides ongoing information about the client's progress. It does not, however, inform the worker about the extent to which any changes in the client's situation relate to the direct practice intervention. It could be that the client or family members would have improved anyway.

More sophisticated (high-level) single case study techniques do attempt to provide information about the extent to which the worker has contributed to the improvement. These generally involve a higher level of intrusion into the direct practice process. For example, the client's situation might be monitored over a period of time before any intervention is offered. This might involve delaying intervention and interviewing the client about the situation a number of times before client–worker contact begins. This at least provides a more meaningful assessment of the original problem against which progress can be compared. Other single case study designs withdraw services for a period of time to assess whether there is some deterioration in the client's progress. If the intervention is contributing to the client's progress, then presumably the progress would be affected by the worker's temporary withdrawal.

These higher-level single case study designs have obvious practical, as well as ethical, problems for most workers with involuntary clients. For the most part, workers are required to deliver services immediately and continuously. The use of higher-level single case study designs has been controversial for this and for other reasons. They have been criticised because workers are reluctant to use them, they do not benefit clients and the results are difficult to interpret (Rubin and Knox 1996). Nonetheless, there is a vast literature on single case study designs and practices of all types, particularly in the United States, where the use of single case study practices has been associated with professional accreditation of social workers.

To sum up, I believe there is a strong argument for workers to routinely seek the opinions of their clients about their progress and about the extent to which the worker is helping. Low- and medium-level single case study evaluations can help to provide this, and can provide a valuable supplement to evidence-based practice as it has been defined in this book.

# Case analysis

Another method by which workers can evaluate their own practice is through case analysis. For the purposes of this discussion, case analysis involves analysing the way a worker is working or has worked with a particular client or client family. It involves reflecting upon and analysing the extent to which the work is consistent with research about what works and about the sources of knowledge which have been drawn upon by the worker.

Outlined below is a series of questions which workers might address in an attempt to analyse the extent to which their work is consistent with evidence-based practice. These questions might also be used in supervision sessions by senior workers to help their staff examine the casework process. The use of similar questions in an exploratory study in a mental health setting resulted in more use of 'effective' practices by workers and higher levels of satisfaction by clients (Harkness and Hensley 1991). If workers can give clear and positive answers to these questions, they are likely to be doing effective work with their clients.

1. What does your client understand to be the purpose of your work with her/him?
2. What have you done to reach agreement with your client about purpose?
3. What does your client hope to achieve from this intervention?
4. Are you working with your client's goals?

5. How will you know if your client is successful in achieving his/her goals?
6. Has the client suggested strategies to achieve the goals?
7. Do you have a contract?
8. What positive comments/actions did you praise or reward in your last interview?
9. Did the rewards or praise you offered substantially out-number the instances of confrontation?
10. What actions/comments did you confront in your last interview?
11. How did you confront those actions/comments?
12. Does the client believe you are helping?

The worker might also reflect upon the extent to which various factors such as values, research findings, organisational expectations, theories or personal experiences have influenced the way they worked with the client. More specifically, the worker might ask: 'What sources of information have I used in my work with this client (e.g. research findings, values, organisational expectations, theories)? Why and how have I used these?' Using these questions, the worker can reflect on the extent to which their practice is consistent with the evidence about what works and on the way in which different sources of knowledge have influenced the way they have worked with the client.

## Critical incidents

A second approach to the analysis of cases, besides analysing the work with a client, involves *critical incidents*. Critical incidents can be defined in different ways. The following definition makes use of work by Ryan, Fook and Hawkins (1995) and Jan Fook (1996). A critical incident relates to a situation which seemed to help the client a lot; which seemed to be most *un*helpful to the client; which the worker found very difficult and caused a lot of anxiety; which gave the worker a great deal of satisfaction; which led to a realisation about the nature of the work; which challenged the worker's beliefs; or which left the worker confused about what they were doing.

Workers might examine critical incidents in terms of why they were critical and how they felt about them at the time. They might also consider the following:

- What knowledge, values, experiences or expectations did you take into account in responding to the situation?
- Are there research findings, or is there other knowledge, which might have helped you deal with the situation better?
- To what extent was your handling of the incident consistent with research about effective practice? Were there, for example, issues relating to role clarification, the values or practices you reinforced, or the extent to which you focused on the client's definition of the problem?
- How would you handle the incident differently if you were in a similar situation again?

These questions might be worked through individually, with a colleague or in supervision.

Case analysis using these sorts of questions can help workers to evaluate their practice and consider how it can be more effective. It complements the lower-level single case study analysis which helps workers to become more effective by monitoring client progress. These approaches in turn complement the use of evidence-based approaches to work with involuntary clients.

# Conclusion

It was pointed out in Chapter 1 that workers with involuntary clients, like others in the welfare sector, often do not make use of research or theory in their work.

The reasons for this are open to speculation. In my own work in probation and child protection, and in brief stints in mental health and in drug rehabilitation, I felt for many years after my graduation in social work that I was working in a theoretical vacuum. It was not that I did not wish to use research findings or theory in my work, it was simply that I was confused about what research findings to use and how to use them. What I learned in a university social work course somehow did not translate into my practice with involuntary clients.

However, as the state of knowledge about effective practice has developed in recent decades, it has became apparent that some practices work better with involuntary clients than others. Even though many workers don't make conscious use of research or theory, some workers clearly are more effective than others.

It is in this context that I have undertaken several studies examining the relationship between worker skills and client outcomes. It is apparent from these studies that when workers make use of certain skills, their clients reoffend less often, abuse their children less often and experience less family breakdown. The positive impact of those workers is not small—in fact, workers with good skills in my studies had clients who were half as likely to go to prison and they also had clients who were twice as likely to be satisfied with child protection outcomes. These results are consistent with what is now becoming a plethora of research which suggests that workers with good skills can make a real and substantial difference to the outcomes for their clients—whether it be in probation, child protection, mental health, drug rehabilitation, youth work or school welfare.

In this book I have tried to present a practice model which is soundly based on research findings, but which takes into account other important sources of knowledge, particularly the values of the worker. I have tried to present it in a way which is jargon-free and accessible to the wide range of people who work with involuntary clients.

It is my hope that this book will influence the practice of those people. And it is my hope that, in turn, something of the day-to-day pain and suffering which is the norm for so many of our clients will be alleviated.

APPENDIX **PRINCIPLES OF EFFECTIVE PRACTICE**

This summary of the principles of effective practice is designed to be displayed in the offices of workers who use this model and to be shared with clients. It aims to provide a reminder to workers about effective practices, and to help familiarise clients with the approach of their worker.

# 1. Role clarification

Involves frequent open and honest discussions about role, for example:

- the purpose of your intervention;
- your dual role as helper/investigator;
- the client's expectations of you;
- your authority and how it can be used;
- negotiable and non-negotiable areas;
- confidentiality (or who can know).

# 2. Pro-social modelling and reinforcement

- Identify behaviours/comments you wish to promote.
- Reward/encourage the comments/behaviours you wish to promote.
- Model the behaviour/comments you wish to promote.
- Identify and discourage or confront comments/behaviours you wish to change.
- Aim for four positives or rewards to every negative or confrontational comment.

# 3. Problem-solving

- Problem survey
- Problem ranking
- Problem exploration
- Setting goals
- Developing a contract
- Developing strategies
- Ongoing monitoring

# 4. Relationship

The worker should:

- be open and honest;
- use empathy;
- challenge rationalisations, not minimise;
- be non-blaming;
- be optimistic;
- articulate client and family members' feelings and problems;
- use appropriate self-disclosure;
- use appropriate humour.

# REFERENCES

Acierno, R., Donohue, B. & Kogan, E. (1994) 'Psychological interventions for drug abuse: a critique and summation of controlled studies', *Clinical Psychology Review* 14:417–42

Adams-Berger, J. (2003) 'Risk and protective factors in relation to substance use and grade differences', *Dissertation Abstracts International A: The Humanities and Social Sciences* 64(3):1073–74

Akers, R.L. (1994) *Criminological Theories—Introduction and Evaluation*, Roxbury Publishing, Los Angeles

Alexander, J., Barton, C., Shiavo, R.S. & Parsons, B.V. (1978) 'Systems behavioural intervention with families of delinquents: therapist characteristics, family behaviour and outcome', *Journal of Consulting and Clinical Psychology* 44:656–64

Alexander, J. & Parsons, B.V. (1973) 'Short-term behavioural intervention with delinquent families: impact on family process and recidivism', *Journal of Consulting and Clinical Psychology* 81:219–25

——(1982) *Functional Family Therapy*, Brooks Cole, Monterey

Allan, J., Pease, B. & Briskman, L. (2003) *Critical Social Work: An Introduction to Theories and Practices*, Allen & Unwin, Sydney

Allison, S., Stacey, S., Dadds, V., Roeger, L., Wood, A. & Martin, G. (2003) 'What the family brings: gathering evidence for strengths-based work', *Journal of Family Therapy* 25:263–84

Anderson, S.C. & Mandell, D.L. (1989) 'The use of self-disclosure by professional social workers', *Social Casework* 70(5):259–67

Andrews, D.A. (1982) *The Level of Supervision Inventory*, Carleton University, Ottawa

——(2001) 'Effective practice: future directions', in D. Andrews, C. Hollin, P. Raynor, C. Trotter & B. Armstrong (eds), *Sustaining Effectiveness in Working with Offenders*, Cognitive Centre Foundation, Cardiff

Andrews, D.A. & Bonta, J. (2003) *The Psychology of Criminal Conduct*, Anderson Publishing, Cincinnati

Andrews, D.A., Keissling, J.J. & Robinson, D. (1986) 'The risk principle of case classification: an outcome evaluation with young adult probationers', *Canadian Journal of Criminology* 28(4):377–84

Andrews, D.A., Keissling, J.J., Russell, R.J. & Grant, B.A. (1979) *Volunteers and the One-to-One Supervision of Adult Probationers*, Ontario Ministry of Correctional Services, Toronto

Andrews, D.A. & Robinson, D. (1984) *The Level of Supervision Inventory: Second Report*, Ontario Ministry of Correctional Services, Ottawa

Andrews, D.A., Zinger, I., Hoge, R., Bonta, J., Gendreau, P. & Cullen, F. (1990) 'Does correctional treatment work? A clinically relevant and psychologically informed meta-analysis', *Criminology* 28(3):369–401

Annis, H.M. (1990) 'Effective treatment for drug and alcohol problems: what do we know?', *Forum on Corrections Research* 2(4):18–24

Baker, M. & Steiner, J. (1995) 'Solution Focused Social Work: Meta-messages to students in higher education opportunity programs', *Social Work* 40(2):225–32

Bandura, A. (1977) 'Self-efficacy: towards a unifying theory of behavioural change', *Psychological Review* 84:191–215

Barber, J. (1991) *Beyond Casework*, Macmillan, Basingstoke

——(1995) 'Working with resistant drug abusers', *Social Work* 40(1):17–23

——(2002) *Social Work with Addictions*, Palgrave Macmillan, Basingstoke

Barton, C. & Alexander, J. (1981) 'Functional family therapy', in A.S. Gurman & P. Kniskern (eds), *Handbook of Family Therapy*, Brunner Mayel, New York

Barton, C., Alexander, J.F., Waldron, H., Turner, C.W. & Warburton, J. (1985) 'Generalising treatment effects of functional family therapy: three replications', *American Journal of Family Therapy* 13:16–26

Beaver, H. (1999) 'Client violence against professional social workers: frequency worker characteristics, and impact on worker job satisfaction burnout and health', *Dissertation Abstracts International A; The Humanities and Social Sciences* 60(6):2227-A

Benjamin, J., Bessant, J. & Watts, R. (1997) *Making Groups Work*, Allen & Unwin, Sydney

Berg, I.K. (1994) *Family-based Practice—A Solution-focused Approach*, W.W. Norton, New York

Berg, I.K. & De Jong, P. (1996) 'Solution-building conversations: co-constructuring a sense of competence with clients', *Families in Society* 77(6):376–91

Berliner, L. (2005) 'The results of randomised clinical trials move the field forward', *Child Abuse and neglect* 29:103–5

Bourgon, G. & Armstrong, B. (2005) 'Transferring the principles of effective treatment into a "real world" setting', *Criminal Justice and Behaviour* 32(1):3–25

Bowie, V. (1996) *Coping with Violence: A Guide for the Human Services*, 2nd edn, Whiting & Birch, London

Briar, S. (1990) 'Empiricism in clinical practice', in L. Videka Sherman & W. Reid (eds), *Advances in Clinical Social Work Practice*, National Association of Social Workers Press, Baltimore

Burns, P. (1994) Pro-social Practices in Community Corrections, Honours thesis, Monash University, Melbourne

Burton, D. & Meezan, W. (2004) 'Revisiting Recent Research on Social Learning Theory as an Etiological Proposition for Sexually Abusive Male Adolescents', *Journal of Evidence-Based Social Work* 1(1):41–80

Carew, R. (1979) 'The place of knowledge in social work activity', *British Journal of Social Work* 9:349–93

Carkhuff, R.R. (1969) *Helping and Human Relations*, Holt Rinehart & Winston, New York

Chaffin, M. & Friedrich, B. (2004) 'Evidence-based treatments in child abuse and neglect', *Children and Youth Services Review* 25(11):1097–113

Cherry, S. (2005) *Transforming Behaviour: Pro-social modelling in practice*, Willan Publishing, Devon

Chestnut, J. (2004) 'Ethics: A touchy subject', *The New Social Worker* 11(1):4

Compton, B. & Galaway, B. (2005) *Social Work Processes*, 6th edn, Dorsey, Homewood

Corcoran, J., 'Family interventions with child physical abuse and neglect: a critical review', *Children and Youth Services Review* 22(7):563–91

Coviello, D., Alterman, A., Rutherford, M., Cacciola, J., Mckay, J. & Zanis, D. (2001) 'The effectivenes of two intensities of psychosocial treatment for drug dependence', *Drug and Alcohol Dependence* 61(2):145–54

Davis, C., Tang, C. & Co, J. (2002) 'Assessing the impact of social factors on the mental health of Chinese at risk adolescents in Hong Kong', *The British Journal of Social Work* 32(5):609–19

DeChillo, N. (1993) 'Collaboration between social workers and families of patients with mental illness', *Families in Society* 74(2):104–15

De Jong, P. & Miller, S. (1996) 'How to interview for client strengths', *Social Work* 40(6):729–36

De Jong, P. & Berg, Insoo K. (2001) 'Co-constructing cooperation with mandated clients', *Social Work* 46(4):361–75

Derlega, V.J. & Berg, J.H. (1987) *Self-Disclosure: Theory Research and Therapy*, Plenum Press, New York

DeShazer, S. (1988) *Clues: Investigating Solutions in Brief Therapy*, W.W. Norton, New York

Doel, M. & Marsh, P. (1992) *Task-centred Social Work*, Ashgate, Aldershot

Dominelli, L. (2002) *Feminist Social Work Theory and Practice*, Palgrave, Hampshire

Dowden, C. & Andrews, D.A. (2004) 'The importance of staff practice in delivering effective correctional treatment: a meta-analytic review of the literature', *International Journal of Offender Therapy and Comparative Criminology* 48(2):203–14

Dungee-Anderson, D. & Beckett, J. (1995) 'A process model for multi-cultural social work practice', *Families in Society* 76(8):459–68

Eaves, C. (2004) 'Heroin use among female adolescents: the role of partner influence, path of initiation and route of administration', *The American Journal of Drug and Alcohol Abuse* 30(1):21–38

Eckstein, D., Junkins, E. & McBrien, R. (2003) 'Ha Ha Ha Improving Couple and Family Humor (Healthy Humor Quotient)', *The family Journal Counselling and Therapy for Couples and Families* 11(3):301–5

Edleson, J. & Syers, M. (1990) 'Relative effectiveness of group treatment for men who batter', *Social Work Research and Abstracts* 26(2):10–17

Epstein, N.B. & Bishop, D.S. (1981) 'Problem-centred systems and the family', in A.S. Gurman & P. Kniskern (eds), *Handbook of Family Therapy*, Brunner Mayel, New York

Farmer, E. (1999) 'Holes in the Safety Net: The strengths and weaknesses of child protection procedures', *Child and family Social Work* 4(4):293–302

Ferguson, J.E. (1983) A neo-Lewinian approach to the identification of mechanisms of change in research with offenders, unpublished PhD thesis, Carleton University, Ottawa

Fischer, J. (1973) 'Is casework effective—a review', *Social Work* 18:5–20

——(1990) 'Problems and issues in meta-analysis', in L. Videka-Sherman & W. Reid (eds), *Advances in Clinical Social Work Research*, National Association of Social Workers Press, Baltimore

Fo, W. & O'Donnell, C. (1974) 'The buddy system: relationship and contingency conditions in a community intervention program for youth with non-professionals as charge agents', *Journal of Consulting and Clinical Psychology*, 42:163–69

Fook, J. (1986) 'Feminist contributions to casework practice', H. Marchand & B. Wearing (eds), in *Gender Reclaimed*, Hale & Iremonger, Sydney

——(1993) *Radical Casework*, Allen & Unwin, Sydney

——(ed.) (1996) *The Reflective Researcher*, Allen & Unwin, Sydney

——(2002) *Social Work: Critical Theory and Practice*, Sage, London

Forgatch, M. & Patterson, G. (1989) *Parents and Adolescents Living Together: Part 1 The Basics; Part 2 Family Problem Solving*, Castalia Publishing, Eugene, Oregon

Fortune, A. (1992) 'Inadequate resources', in W. Reid (ed.), *Task Strategies: An Empirical Approach to Clinical Social Work*, Columbia University Press, New York

Furstenberg, A.L. & Rounds, K.A. (1995) 'Self-efficacy as a target for social work intervention', *Families in Society* 6(9):587–95

Gendreau, P. (1996) 'The principles of effective intervention with offenders', in A.T. Harland (ed.), *Choosing Correctional Options That Work*, Sage, Newbury Park

Gendreau, P., Little, T. & Goggin, C. (1996) 'A meta-analysis of the predictors of adult recidivism: what works!', *Criminology* 34:575–607

Germain, C.B. & Gitterman, A. (1996) *The Life Model of Social Work Practice: Advances in Theory and Practice*, Columbia University Press, New York

Gibbs, J. (2001) 'Maintaining front line workers in child protection: a case for refocusing supervision', *Child Abuse Review* 10(5):323–35

Gillham, J. and Reivich, J. (2004) 'Cultivating optimism in childhood and adolescence', *The Annals of the American Academy* 591:146–63

Gilligan, R. (2001) *Promoting Resilience: A Resource Guide on Working with Children in the Care System*, British Agencies for Adoption and Fostering, London

Gingerich, S.L. & Bellack, A.S. (1996) 'Research-based family interventions for the treatment of schizophrenia', *Research on Social Work Practice* 6(1):122–26

Goldenberg, I. & Goldenberg, H. (2004) *Family Therapy: An overview*, 6th edn, Brooks/Cole Pacific Grove, California

Goldstein, E. (1995) *Ego Psychology and Social Work Practice*, 2nd edn, Free Press, New York

Gordon, D.A. & Arbuthnot, J. (1990) 'Promising approaches for chronic juvenile offenders: interventions with the family and other social systems', paper presented at the annual convention of the American Society of Criminology, Baltimore

Gordon, D.A., Arbuthnot, J., Gustafson, K.E. & McGreen, P. (1988) 'Home-based behavioural systems: family therapy with disadvantaged juvenile delinquents', *American Journal of Family Therapy* 16(3):243–55

Gottschalk, L. (1973) 'A study of prediction and outcome in a mental health crisis clinic', *American Journal of Psychiatry* 130:1107–11

Gough, D. (1993) *Child Abuse Interventions—A Review of the Research Literature*, Public Health Research Unit, University of Glasgow, Her Majesties Stationary Office, London

Gough, H.G. (1960) 'Theory and measurement of socialisation', *Journal of Consulting Psychology* 24(1):23–30

Grant, A. (ed.) (2004) *Cognitive Behavioural Therapy in Mental Health Care*, Sage, London

Gursansky, D., Harvey, J. & Kennedy, R. (2003) *Case Management Policy Practice and Professional Business*, Allen & Unwin, Sydney

Harkness, D. & Hensley, H. (1991) 'Changing the focus of social work super-vision: effects on client satisfaction and generalised contentment', *Social Work* 36(6):506–12

Heffernan, J., Shuttlesworth, G. & Ambrosino, R. (1997) *Social Work and Social Welfare: An Introduction*, West Publishing Company, New York

Hepworth, D.H., Rooney, R.R. & Larson, J.A. (2002) *Direct Social Work Practice*, Brooks Cole, Pacific Grove, California

Hinton, W.J., Sherpis, C. & Sims, P. (2003) 'Family based approaches to juvenile delinquency: a review of the literature', *The Family Journal: Counselling and therapy for couples and families* 11:2:167–73

Her Majesties Stationary Office (HMSO) (1995) *Child Protection: Messages From Research*, HMSO, London

Hodges, J., Hardiman, E. & Segal, S. (2003) 'Predictors of hope among members of mental health self help agencies', *Social Work in Mental Health* 2(1):1–16

Hogan, R. (1969) 'Development of an empathy scale', *Journal of Consulting Psychology* 34(3):307–16

Hohman, M. (1998) 'Motivational interviewing: an intervention tool for child welfare case workers working with substance abusing parents' *Child Welfare* 77(3):275–89

Holder, R. & Salovitz, B. (2001) *Child Safety and Child Neglect: National Resource Centre on child maltreatment*, Duluth, GA

Ife, J. (1997) *Rethinking Social Work*, Longman, Melbourne

Ivanoff, A., Blythe, B. & Tripodi, T. (1994) *Involuntary Clients in Social Work Practice*, Aldine de Gruyter, New York

Jacobs, D. (2003) 'The coping skills of child protection workers exposed to prim or secondary trauma in the workplace', *Dissertation Abstracts International A: The Humanities and Social Sciences* 64:6

Jones, J.A. & Alcabes, A. (1993) *Client Socialisation: The Achilles Heel of the Helping Professions*, Auburn House, Westport, Connecticut

Keissling, J.J. (1982) *The Problem Solving Dimension in Correctional Counselling*, Ontario Ministry of Correctional Services, Ottawa

Kerson, T. *(2002) Boundary Spanning: An Ecological Reinterpretation of Social Work Practice in Health and Mental Health Systems*, Columbia University Press, New York

Kirk, S.A. & Koeske, G.F. (1995) 'The fate of optimism: a longitudinal study of case managers' hopefulness and subsequent morale', *Research on Social Work Practice* 5(1):47–61

Kolko, D. (2002) 'Child physical abuse', in J.E.B. Myers, L. Berliner, J. Briere & C.T. Hendrix (eds), *The APSAC Handbook on Child Maltreatment*, 2nd edn, Sage Publications, Thousand Oaks, CA

Laming, Lord (2003) 'The Victoria Climbie Inquiry Speech', www.victoria-climbie-inquiry.org.uk

LaSala, M. (1997) 'Client satisfaction: consideration of correlates and response bias', *Families in Society* 78(1):54–62

Lee, Frances Wing-Lin & Mui-Ling, Fanny (2003) 'Young School Dropouts: Levels of influence of different systems', *Journal of Youth Studies* 6:1:89–110

Letendre, J. (1999) 'Lender and therapeutic influences on aggressive behaviours and pro-social skills in groups with children', *Dissertation Abstracts International A: The Humanities and Social Sciences* 60(6):2228-A

Lipsey, M.W. (1991) 'Juvenile delinquency treatment: a meta-analytic inquiry into the variability of effects', in T.D. Cook, H. Cooper, D.S. Corday, H. Hartmann et al. (eds), *MetaAnalysis for Explanation: A Casebook*, Russell Sage Foundation, New York

Littlechild, B. (2002) 'The effects of client violence on child protection networks', *Trauma Violence and Abuse* 3(2):144–58

Loneck, B. (1995) 'Getting persons with alcohol and other drug problems into treatment: teaching the Johnson intervention in the practice curriculum', *Journal of Teaching in Social Work* 11(1–2):31–44

Longshore, D., Turner, S. & Fain, T. (2005) 'Effects of case management on parolee misconduct', *Criminal Justice and Behaviour* 32(4):205–22

Luiselli, J., Cannon, B., Ellis, J. & Sisson, R. (2000) 'Home based behavioural therapy for children with autism/pervasive developmental disorder: a preliminary evaluation of outcome in relation to child age and intensity of service delivery', *Autism* 4(4):426–38

Lurigio, A. (2000) 'Drug treatment availability and effectiveness studies of the general and criminal justice populations', *Criminal Justice and Behaviour* 27(4):495–528

Majer, J., Jason, L., Ferrari, J., Olson, B. & North, C. (2003) 'Is self mastery always a helpful resource?', *American Journal of Drug and Alcohol Abuse* 29:2:385–399

Markiewicz, A. (1994) 'How social workers survive in public welfare: training for best practice in a declassified, increasingly narrowly administrative context', *Advances in Social and Welfare Education*, University of Western Australia, Perth

Marsh, P. (2004) *The Task Centred Book: Developing, Learning, Sustaining and Reviewing Task Centred Social Work*, Taylor & Francis, London

Masters, J., Thomas, G., Hollon, S. & Rimm, D. (1987) *Behaviour Therapy*, Harcourt Brace, Fort Worth

McDonald, G. (2001) *Effective Interventions in Child Abuse and Neglect*, Wiley, Chichester, UK

McIvor, G. (1992) *Sentenced to Serve*, Avebury, London

McMahon, A. (1998) *Damned if You Do, Damned if You Don't*, Ashgate, Aldershot

Milgram, D. & Rubin, J. (1992) 'Resisting resistance; involuntary substance abuse group therapy', *Social Work with Groups* 15(1):95–110

Miller, P., Herson, M., Eisler, R. & Watts, J. (1974) 'Contingent reinforcement of lowered blood/alcohol levels in an outpatient chronic alcoholic', *Behaviour Research and Therapy* 12:261–63

Moore, K.J., Greenfield, W.L., Wilson, M. & Kok, A. (1997) 'Toward a taxonomy of batterers', *Families in Society* 78(6):353–60

Moos, R. & Moos, B. (2003) 'Long term influence of duration and intensity of treatment on first episode and untreated', *Addiction* 98(3):325–37

Morley, C. (2003) 'Critical reflection in social work: a response to globalisation', *International Journal of Social Welfare* 13:297–303

Moyers, T. & Rollnick, S. (2002) 'A motivational interviewing perspective on resistance to therapy', *JCLP/In session: Psychotherapy in Practice* 58(2):185–193

Mullaly, R. (2002) *Challenging Oppression: A critical social work approach*, Oxford University Press, Ontario

Mullen, D. & Steiner, D. (2004) 'The evidence for and against evidence based practice', *Brief Treatment and Crisis Intervention* 4:2:111–21

Mullender, A. (1996) *Rethinking Domestic Violence*, Routledge, London

Murdach, A.D. (1996) 'Beneficence re-examined: protective intervention in mental health', *Social Work* 41(1):26–32

Newell, C. (2003) *Client Violence in Social Work Practice: Prevention, Intervention and Research*, The Guildford Press, New York

Newhill, C.E. (1996) 'Prevalence and risk factors for client violence towards social workers', *Families in Society* 77(8):488–96

Nugent, W.R. & Halvorson, H. (1995) 'Testing the effects of active listening', *Research on Social Work Practice* 5(2):152–75

O'Connor, I., Wilson, J. and Setterlund, D. (1996) 'Readiness for change: variation by intensity and domain of client distress', *Social Work Research* 20(1):13–18

——(2003) *Social Work and Welfare Practice*, Pearson Longman, Melbourne

O'Hare, T. (1991) 'Integrating research and practice: a framework for implementation', *Social Work* 36(3):220–23

Owen, L. & Richards, D. (1995) 'Social work and corrections', in P. Swain (ed.), *In the Shadow of the Law*, Federation Press, Sydney

Pearson, F., Lipton, D., Cleland, C. & Yee, D. (2002) 'The effects of behavioural/cognitive behavioural programs on recidivism', *Crime and Delinquency* 48(3):476–96

Perkins, D. & Jones, K. (2004) 'Risk behaviours and resiliency within physically abused adolescents', *Child Abuse and Neglect* 28(5):547–63

Perkins-Dock, R. (2001) 'Family interventions with incarcerated youth: a review of the literature', *International Journal of Offender Therapy and Comparative Criminology* 45(5):606–25

Perlman, H.H. (1957) *Social Casework: A Problem Solving Process*, University of Chicago Press, Chicago

Polkki, O., Ervast, S. and Huupponen, M. (2004) 'Coping and resilience of children of a mentally ill parent', *Social Work in Health Care* 39(1–2):151–63

Pollio, D.E. (1995) 'Use of humour in crisis intervention', *Families in Society* 76(6):376–84

Puckett, T.C. & Cleak, H. (1994) 'Caution—helping may be hazardous: client abuse, threats and assaults', *Australian Social Work* 47(1):3–10

Raynor, P. (2003) 'Research in probation: from nothing works to what works', in Wing Hong Chui and M. Nellis (eds), *Moving Probation Forward: Evidence, Arguments and Practice*, Pearson Longman, London

Raynor, P. & Vanstone, M. (1996) 'Reasoning and rehabilitation in Britain: the results of the Straight Thinking on Probation (STOP) programme',

*International Journal of Offender Therapy and Comparative Criminology* 40(4):272–84

Reid, W. (1985) *Family Problem Solving*, Columbia University Press, New York

——(1992) *Task Strategies: An Empirical Approach to Clinical Social Work*, Columbia University Press, New York

——(1994) 'The empirical practice movement', *Social Service Review* 68(2):163–84

——(1997a) 'Evaluating the dodo's verdict: do all interventions have equivalent outcomes?', *Social Work Research* 21(1):5–16

——(1997b) 'Research on task-centred practice', *Social Work Research* 21(3):134–37

Reid, W. & Epstein, L. (1972) *Task-centred Casework*, Columbia University Press, New York

Reid, W. & Hanrahan, P. (1982) 'Recent evaluations of social work: grounds for optimism', *Social Work* 27:328–40

Reid, W. & Shyne, A. (1969) *Brief and Extended Casework*, Columbia University Press, New York

Rex, S. and Gelsthorpe, L. (2002) 'The role of community service in reducing offending: evaluating pathfinder projects in the UK', *The Howard Journal* 41(4):311–25

Rey, L.D. (1996) 'What social workers need to know about client violence', *Families in Society* 77(1):33–39

Roberts, C. (1993) *What Works: Using Social Work Methods to Reduce Reoffending in Serious and Persistent Offenders*, Social Work Department, Oxford University, Oxford

Robinson, G. (2003) 'Risk and risk Assessment' in Wing Hong Chui & M. Nellis *Moving Probation Forward Evidence Arguments and Practice*, Pearson Longman, London UK

Rooney, R. (1992) *Strategies for Work with Involuntary Clients*, Columbia University Press, New York

Rothman, J. (1991) 'A model of case management: toward empirically based practice', *Social Work* 36(6):337–43

Rubin, A. (1985) 'Practice effectiveness: more grounds for optimism', *Social Work* 30:469–76

Rubin, A. & Babbie, E. (2005) *Research Methods for Social Work*, Thomson Brooks/Cole, Belmont

Rubin, A. & Knox, K. (1996) 'Data analysis problems in single case evaluation: issues for research on social work practice', *Research on Social Work Practice* 6(1):40–65

Ryan, M., Fook, J. & Hawkins, L. (1995) 'From beginner to graduate social worker: preliminary findings of an Australian longitudinal study', *British Journal of Social Work* 25(1):17–35

Ryan, M., Merighi, R., Healy, B. & Renouf, N. (2004) 'Belief optimism and caring: findings from a cross national study of expertise in mental health social work', *Qualitative Social Work* 3(4):411–29

Saleebey, D. (2001) 'Practicing the strengths perspective: everyday tools and resources', *Families in Society: The Journal of Contemporary Human Services* 82:3

Schepker, R., Grabbe, Y. & Jahn, K.A. (2003) 'Longitudinal view on inpatient treatment duration: is there a lower limit to length of stay in child and adolescent psychiatry', *Praxis Der Kinderpsychologie Und Kinderpsychiatrie* 52(5):338–53

Schwalbe, C. (2004) 'Re-visioning risk assessment for human service decision making', *Children and Youth Services Review* 26(6):561–76

Scott, D. & O'Neill, D. (1996) *Beyond Child Rescue*, Allen & Unwin, Sydney

Scourfield, J. (2002) 'Reflections of gender knowledge and values in social work', *British Journal of Social Work* 32:1–15

Searing, H. (2003) 'The continuing relevance of casework ideas to long term child protection work', *Child and Family Social Work* 8:311–20

Seligman, M. (1990) *Learned Optimism*, Random House, Sydney

——(1995) *The Optimistic Child*, Random House, Sydney

Selman, D., Sullivan, J., Dore, G., Adamson, S. & MacEwan, I. (2001) 'The randomized controlled trial of motivational enhancement therapy for mild to moderate alcohol dependence', *Journal of Studies on Alcohol* 62(3):389–96

Sexton, T. & Alexander, J. (2002) 'Family based empirically supported interventions', *The Counseling Psychologist* 30(2):238–61

Sheldon, B. (1987) 'Implementing findings from social work effectiveness research', *British Journal of Social Work* 17:573–86

Shlonsky, A. & Gibbs, L. (2004) 'Will the real evidence based practice please step forward: teaching the process of EBP to the helping professions', *Journal of Brief Therapy and Crisis Intervention* 4(2):137–53

Shlonsky, A. & Wagner, D. (2005) 'The next step: Integrating actuarial risk assessment and clinical judgement into an evidence based practice framework in CPS case management', *Children and Youth Services Review* 27:409–27

Shulman, L. (1991) *Interactional Social Work Practice: Toward an Empirical Theory*, F.E. Peacock, Itasca, Illinois

Siporin, M. (1984) 'Have you heard the one about social work humour?', *Social Casework* 68(8):459–64

Slawinski, T. (2004) 'The intensive case manager–client relationship: understanding and influencing boundary development and compliance', *Dissertation Abstracts International A: The Humanities and Social Sciences* 64:9

Smokowski, P. & Wodarski, J. (1996) 'Effectiveness of child welfare services', *Research on Social Work Practice* 6(4):504–23

Spratt, T. & Houston, S. (1999) 'Developing critical social work in theory and in practice: child protection and communicative reason', *Child and Family Social Work* 4(4):315–27

Stanley, J. & Goddard, C. (2002) *In the Firing Line*, Wiley, Chichester

Steib, S. & Blome, W. (2004) 'Fatal error: the missing ingredient in child welfare reform part 2', *Child Welfare* 83(1):101–4

Strozier, A., Krizek, C. & Sale, K. (2003) 'Touch: its use in psychotherapy', *Journal of Social Work Practice* 17(1):49–62

Thomlinson, R. (1984) 'Something works: evidence from practice effectiveness studies', *Social Work* 29(1):51–56

Thorpe, D. (1994) *Evaluating Child Protection*, Open University Press, Buckingham

Trotter, C. (1990) 'Probation can work: a research study using volunteers', *Australian Journal of Social Work* 43(2):13–18

——(1993) The effective supervision of offenders, unpublished PhD thesis, La Trobe University, Melbourne

——(1994) 'Task-centred social work—an interview with William Reid', *Advances in Social Work Education* 2:3–5

——(1995b) 'Contamination theory and unpaid community work', *Australian and New Zealand Journal of Criminology* 28(2):163–75

——(1995a) *The Supervision of Offenders: What Works? First and Second Reports to the Criminology Research Council*, Department of Social Work, Monash University, and Department of Justice, Melbourne

——(1996b) 'Community corrections—punishment or welfare: a book review essay', *International Criminal Justice Review* 6:121–30

——(1996a) 'The impact of different supervision practices in community corrections', *Australian and New Zealand Journal of Criminology* 29(1):29–46

——(1997b) *Family Problem Solving—Report to Vic Safe*, Department of Social Work, Monash University, Melbourne

——(1997a) 'Working with mandated clients—a pro-social approach', *Australian Journal of Social Work* 50(2):19–27

——(2000) 'Teaching family work: integrating teaching practice and research', *Advances in Social Work and Welfare Education* 3(1):161–70

——(2002) 'Worker style and client outcome in child protection', *Child Abuse Review* 11:38–50

——(2004) *Helping Abused Children and Their Families*, Allen & Unwin/Sage, Sydney and London

Trotter, C., Cox, D. & Crawford, K. (2002) 'Family Counselling in Juvenile Justice', *Australian Social Work* 55(1):119–27

Trotter, C. & Sheehan, R. (2005) 'Women's access to welfare after prison', conference paper presented to What Works with Women Offenders, Monash University, Prato, Italy

Truax, C.B., Wargo, D.G. & Sibler, L.D. (1966) 'Effects of group psychotherapy with high accurate empathy and non-possessive warmth upon female institutionalised delinquents', *Journal of Abnormal Psychology* 71(4):267–74

Vanstone, M. (2004) 'A history of the use of groups in probation work: part two—from negotiated treatment to evidence-based practice in an accountable service', *The Howard Journal* 43(2):180–202

Videka Sherman, L. (1988) 'Meta-analysis of research on social work practice in mental health', *Social Work* 33(4):323–38

Waterson, L. & Carnie, J. (1992) 'Assessing child protection risk', *British Journal of Social Work* 22:47–60

Watt, B., Howells, K. & Delfabbro, P. (2004) 'Juvenile Recidivism: Criminal propensity, social control and social learning theories', *Psychiatry, Psychology and Law* 11(1):141–53

White, M. & Epston, D. (1989) *Narrative Means to Therapeutic Ends*, Dulwich Centre Publications, Adelaide

Wilson, D., Bouffard, L. & Mackenzie, D. (2005) 'A Quantitative Review Of Structured, Group-Oriented, Cognitive-Behavioral Programs For Offenders', *Criminal Justice and Behaviour* 32(2):172–204

Wing Hong, Chui & Nellis, M. (eds) (2003) *Moving Probation Forward: Evidence, Arguments and Practice*, Pearson Longman, Essex

Wood, M. (1978) 'Casework effectiveness: a new look at the research evidence', *Social Work* 23(6):437–59

Yip, K., Ngan, M. & Lam, I. (2002) 'An explorative study of peer influence and response to adolescent self cutting behaviour in Hong Kong', *Smith College Studies in Social Work* 72(3):379–401

Zhang, Z., Friedman, P. & Gerstein, D. (2003) 'Does retention matter? Treatment duration and improvement in drug use', *Addiction* 98(5):673–84

# INDEX

actuarial risk assessments  48
Adams-Berger, J.  49
Akers, R.L.  7, 50, 57
Alexander, J. and Parsons, P.V.
    42–3, 114
Alexander, J., Barton, C., Shiavo,
    R.S. and Parson, B.V.  43, 149
Allison, S., Stacey, S., Dadds, V.,
    Roeger, L., Wood, A. and Martin,
    G.  62, 131
Anderson, S.C. and Mandell, D.L.
    153
Andrews, D.A  7, 12, 21, 24, 26, 32,
    41, 47, 88–9, 103, 143
Andrews, D.A. and Bonta, J.  11, 13,
    19, 20, 47, 48, 50, 52, 57, 65, 88,
    94, 114, 122, 126, 131
Andrews, D.A., Keissling, J.J.,
    Russell, R.J. and Grant, B.A.  54,
    55, 88, 98, 99, 102–3, 143
anti-social comments  95

approaches
    what doesn't work 53–4
    what works 21–53
assessment  109, 111
attending for appointments  91
attitudes  104

Bandura, A.  36–7
Barber, J.  24, 26
Barton, C., Alexander, J.F., Waldron,
    H., Turner, C.W. and Warburton,
    J.  43
Beaver, H.  155
behavioural principles  88
behaviourist theory  57
behaviours and attitudes  93
Berg, I.K. and De Jong, P.  111
Berliner, L.  10
blame  53
body language  95
brainstorming in family work  171–2

Burns, P. 92, 95, 96, 98, 99
Burton, D. and Meezan, W. 88

California Personality Inventory 25
Carew, R. 8
Carkhuff, R.R. 32, 144, 152
case analysis 187–8
case management 5–6, 39–42,
    129–30
  criticisms of 39–41
  principles 42
case planning 5–6, 39–42, 129
case studies 80–5, 105–7, 137–40,
    174–9
casework 5
  effectiveness 18–19
Chaffin, M. and Friedrich, B. 8, 9
challenging undesirable behaviours
    95–7, 105
  in family work 174
Cherry, S. 54
Chestnut, J. 146
client evaluations 183
client monitoring forms 184–5
clinical practice 5
cognitive behavioural models 123
cognitive behavioural treatment 57
Cognitive Centre Foundation 123
cognitive theory 57
collaborative family counselling 44,
    161–2
  process 163–73
collaborative problem-solving 25–7
common problems in family work
    167
community resources 39–42
community work 25, 50
Compton, B. and Galaway, B. 25,
    31, 32, 52, 109

confidentiality 71–3
  in family work 164
confrontation 96, 105
  in family work 174
constructive humour 150–1
continuity of service 41
contracts 117–18, 169
Corcoran, J. 26
Coviello, D., Alterman, A.,
    Rotherford, M., Cacciola, J.,
    Mckay, J. and Zanis, D. 46
Cox, D. *see* Trotter, C. studies
Crawford, K. *see* Trotter, C. studies
criminogenic needs 41
crisis situations 83, 125, 168
critical incidents 188–9
critical reflection 60
critical theory 59–61, 103–4
culture 104–5, 146, 163–4

Davis, C., Tang, C. and Co., J. 49
De Jong, P. and Berg, I.K. 2
De Jong, P. and Miller, S. 148
Derlega, V.J. and Berg, J.H. 153
dependency 76
DeShazer, S. 112, 131
destructive humour 151–2
direct practice 5–6
directing clients 135
Doel, M. and Marsh, P. 61, 109
Dominelli, L. 57–8, 103
Dowden, C. and Andrews, D.A. 25,
    30, 36, 54
drug-addicted clients 135–6
drug and alcohol abuse 44
dual role 3–4, 67–9
duration of problem-solving 114
duration of treatment 45–7

Eckstein, D. 150
Eckstein, D., Junkins, E. and
    McBrien, R. 35
ecological systems theory 56–7
effective practice principles 191–2
empathic responses 144–5
empathy 25, 29, 32–5, 143–4
    and pro-social modelling 35
    scales 144
empirical practice 8
encouragement 98
Epstein, N.B. and Bishop, D.S. 161
evaluation 182
evidence-based practice 8–10
    advantages of 13–15
    criticisms of 10–13
    definition 8–10
    limitations 181–2
expectation 37
expectations of client 74–5

family definition 158
    when to work with 159–60
family behavioural therapy 44
family problem-solving 44
family work 42–5, 158–80
family work preparation 163–4
Farmer, E. 12, 127
feminist theory 57–8, 103–4f
Ferguson, J. 51, 123
file notes 72, 93
Fischer, J. 18–19, 22, 114
Fook, J. 57–8, 182, 188
Forgatch, M. and Patterson, G. 161
Fortune, A. 41, 54
frequency of treatment 46
friend/professional role 76
functional family therapy 43
Furstenberg, A.L. and Rounds, K.A.
    149

Gendreau, P. 49, 53, 122
Germain, C.B. and Gitterman, A.
    56
Gibbs, J. 155
Gillham, J. and Reivich, J. 36
Gilligan, R. 62
goals 27, 53–4, 101, 116–17
    client goals 101–2
    in family work 169, 170
    worker goals 101–2
Goldenberg, I. and Goldenberg, H.
    161
Gordon, D.A. and Arbuthnot, J. 43
Gordon, D.A., Arbuthnot, J.,
    Gustafson, K.E. and McGreen, P.
    43
Gottschalk, L. 37
Gough, D. 12, 24, 53, 114
Grant, A. 57
ground rules in family work 165,
    170
groupwork 50–1, 122–4
guidelines for the use of humour
    150
Guransky, D. 5, 42

Harkness, D. and Hensley, H. 182,
    187
Heffernan, J., Shuttlesworth, G. and
    Ambrosino, R. 102
helping clients to manage feelings
    34
helping role 4, 68
Hepworth, D.H., Rooney, R.R, and
    Larson, J.A. 25, 32, 38, 57, 98,
    109, 144
high-risk clients 47–9, 126
higher level case study designs 186
Hinton, W.J., Sherpis, C. and Sims,
    P. 42

Hodges, J., Hardimann, E. and
  Segal, S. 37
Hogan, R. 143
Hohman, M. 62
Holder, R. and Salovitz, B. 127
home-based work with families
  162–3
home tasks in family work 172
hope 37, 147–9
humour 35–6, 149–52

individual problems in family work
  167, 168
insight 53
intellectually disabled clients 135–6
investigatory role 68
involuntary clients 52
  definition 2–3
  examples 2–3
isolated clients 77
Ivanoff, A., Blythe, B. and Tripodi,
  T. 2, 16, 33, 79

Jacobs, D. 36
Jones, J.A. and Alcabes, A. 22, 26,
  46, 52, 54, 65, 131, 132
judgmental comments 29
judgments 98

Keissling, J.J. 96, 116
Kerson, T. 57
Kirk, S. and Koeske, G. 37
Kolko, D. 26

Laming, L. 40
LaSala, M. 183
learning theory 88
Lee, F. and Mui-Ling, F. 49
legal requirements 69–70
Letendre, J. 24

letters 93
Level of Service Inventory—revised
  126
life experience 7
Lipsey, M.W. 53, 122
listening skills in family work 171
Littlechild, B. 154, 155
Loneck, B. 44, 52
long-term interventions 46
Longshore, D., Turner, S. and Fain,
  T. 46
low-risk clients 126
Luiselli, J., Cannon, B., Ellis, J. and
  Sisson, R. 46
Lurigio, A. 46

Majer, J., Jason, L., Ferrari, J.,
  Olson, B. and North, C. 37
mandated clients 2
Markiewicz, A. 5
Marsh, P. 61, 109
Masters, J. 23
Masters, J., Thomas, G., Hollon, S.
  and Rimm, D. 54, 94
McDonald, G. 20
McIvor, G. 50
McMahon, A. 5
meta-analysis 22
Milgram, D. and Rubin, J. 51, 123
Miller, P. et al. 24
minimisation 149
model of practice 54
modelling pro-social behaviours
  93–5
Moore, K.J., Greenfield, W.L.,
  Wilson, M. and Kok, A. 51
Moos, R. and Moos, B. 46
moralising 105
Morely, C. 59, 60
motivation 51–3

motivational interviewing 62–3
Moyers, T. and Rollnick, S. 62
Mullaly, R. 103
Mullen, D. and Steiner, D. 10
Mullender, A. 50
multi-systemic therapy 44

narrative 61
negotiable aspects of the
intervention 69–71, 130
Newell, C. 157
non-blaming expressions in family
work 166
non-negotiable aspects of the
intervention 69, 130
Nugent, W. and Halvorson, H. 33

obstacles to task completion 120
O'Connor, I., Wilson, J. and
Setterlund, D. 32
O'Hare, T. 52
O'Neill, D. 112
optimism 36–7, 147–9
organisational expectations 7–8, 78
organisational policies 78
organisational requirements 69–70
outcomes 10, 14
Owen, L. and Richards, D. 70

paraphrasing in family work 143,
171
parent training 44
partialising problems 112
Pearson, F., Lipton, D., Cleland, C.
and Yee, D. 123
peer group association 49–50, 123
Perkins, D. and Jones, K. 49
Perkins-Dock, R. 44, 162
pessimism 148
political action 136–7

Polkki, O., Ervast, S. and
Huupponen, M. 26, 54
Pollio, D. 35, 150, 151
positive feedback in family work
171
post-modern 59
power differential in family work
162, 165
practice models 7
practice wisdom 7
praise 91, 149
problem exploration 115–16
in work with families 168–9
problem-ranking 112–15
in work with families 167–8
problem-solving 6, 25–7, 29–31,
109–41, 161–73
contract 118
criticisms 130–7
follow through 134
lack of problems 132–4
negative focus 131–2
steps 110
supports status quo 136–7
problem-solving contract and case
plan 129–30
problem-solving display 79, 109,
110
in family work 165
problem survey 110–11, 125
client lists 128, 133, 167
with families 165–7
worker lists 128, 133
progress reports 93
pro-social 87–108
advantages of 98
approach 55
behaviours 90
comments 89
criticisms 98–105

definition 23
judgmental 102
manipulative 100
model 54
modelling 23–5, 29–31, 93–5
practice 54–5
reinforcement 23–5, 29–31
steps 89
superficiality 100
pro-social modelling in family work
173–4
psychiatrically ill clients 135–6
psycho-analytic approaches 114
Puckett, T. and Cleak, H. 155
punishment 53, 88

rating scale for general family
functioning 185
rating scale for problems 184
rationalisations 95
Raynor, P. 123
reaching inside of silences 34
readiness to change 52
real problems 132
referrals 121–2
reflective listening 32–5, 143–4
re-framing 166
Reid, W. 8, 19, 44, 45, 55, 61, 109,
119, 120, 131, 134, 161
Reid, W. and Epstein, L. 61, 109
Reid, W. and Hanrahan, P. 25, 131
Reid, W. and Shyne, A. 45
reinforcing pro-social values 23–25
relationship 31–5, 76–7, 142–57
in family work 174
research 7, 55–56
resilience 62
resources to address problems 168
review of progress 77, 124
in family work 173

rewards 88
intrinsic 88
provision of 91
variable 88
Rex, S. and Gelsthorpe, L. 25
Rey, L.D. 155
rights and rewards 92
risk assessment 47–9, 111
and clinical judgment 125
and investigation 125–7
and problem-solving 127
criticisms of 127
profiles 125
Roberts, C. 50
Robinson, G. 47, 127
role as case manager, case planner or
problem-solver 73–4
role clarification 21–2, 29–31, 65–86
role clarification with families
164–5
role play in family work 171
role-related issues 66
Rooney, R. 2, 16
Rothman, J. 42
Rounds, K. 37
Rubin, A. 25–6, 41, 54, 114, 116,
131
Rubin, A. and Babbie, E. 182
Rubin, A. and Knox, K. 186
Ryan, M., Fook, J. and Hawkins, L.
8, 188
Ryan, M., Merighi, R., Healy, B.
and Renouf, N. 37

Saleebey, D. 61, 131
Schepker, R., Grabbe, Y. and Jahn,
K.A. 46
Schwalbe, C. 48, 125–6
Scott, D. and O'Neill, D. 149
Scourfield, J. 8

Searing, H. 5
self-efficacy 36, 149
self-disclosure 38–9, 94, 152–4
  and modelling 153
  and role clarification 153
Seligman, M. 36, 148
Selman, D., Sullivan, J., Dore, G.
  Adamson, S. and MacEwan, I.
  34, 53
Sexton, T. and Alexander, J. 43, 44,
  160, 162
Sheehan, R. see Trotter, C. studies
Sheldon, B. 25, 116, 131
Shlonsky, A. and Gibbs, L. 9
Shlonsky, A. and Wagner, D. 48
short-term interventions 45
Shulman, L. 21, 26, 34, 35, 38, 54,
  65, 68, 69, 78, 94, 96, 152
single case study evaluation 182–7
Slawinski, T. 40
Smokowski, P. and Wodarski, J. 9,
  26
social and political context 148
social learning theory 24, 57
socialisation 22
solution focused 61–2
solvable problems 167
sources of knowledge 6–8
Spratt, T. and Houston, S. 59, 60
Stanley, J. and Goddard, C. 155
Steib, S. and Blome, W. 40
strategic family therapy 44
strategies and tasks 118–21
  in work with families 171–3
strengths based 61–2, 131, 148
strengths cards 149
Strozier, A., Krizek, C. and Sale, K.
  146
superficiality of pro-social approach
  100

supervision through case analysis
  187
  through critical incidents 189
surveillance role 4
systems theory 56–7

task-centred practice 61
tasks 118–21, 171–3
termination 77
theoretical approach 79
theories 6, 15, 56
Thomlinson, R. 45, 54
Thorpe, D. 4
time-limited interventions 45
touching 146–7
Trotter, C. studies 11, 19, 24–5,
  27–31, 33, 34, 41, 44, 48, 49, 52,
  76, 153, 162
Truax, C.B., Wargo, D.G. and Sibler,
  L.D. 32

values and beliefs 7, 160
Vanstone, M. 51, 123
Videka Sherman, L. 22, 44, 51, 52,
  54, 114, 116, 123, 131
violence by clients 154
  strategies to avoid violence 155–6
voluntary clients 2–3, 52

Watt, B., Howells, K. and
  Delfabbro, P. 88
White, M. and Epston, D. 62, 131
Wilson, D. Bouffard, L. and
  Mackenzie, D. 26, 50, 57
Wing Hong, C. and Nellis, M. 98
Wood, M. 114
worker aims and objectives 12–13
worker honesty 22
worker impact 19–20

worker judgment 182
worker neutrality in family work
173–4
worker reliability 94
worker requirements 69–70
worker safety 154–7, 162
worker values 102–3

workers do this anyway 99–100
written lists in family work 166

Yip, K., Ngan, M. and Lam, I. 49

Zhang, Z., Friedman, P. and
Gerstein, D. 46